Superlife

Superlife

The 7 Steps That Spell S.U.C.C.E.S.S.

Anne Naylor

Thorsons

An Imprint of HarperCollins*Publishers*

Thorsons
An Imprint of HarperCollins*Publishers*
77–85 Fulham Palace Road,
Hammersmith, London W6 8JB

Published by Thorsons 1992
3 5 7 9 10 8 6 4

© Anne Naylor 1992

Anne Naylor asserts the moral right to
be identified as the author of this work

A catalogue record for this book
is available from the British Library

ISBN 0 7225 2600 8

Typeset by Harper Phototypesetters Limited,
Northampton, England
Printed in Great Britain by
HarperCollinsManufacturing Glasgow

Dedication

To Paddy

Contents

About The Author

Anne Naylor has been involved in self-development work for many years. Formerly, she lived in London where she ran seminars and courses for well-known companies, helping executives to effect specific change in their careers and personal relationships. Her particular skill is in showing people how to get in touch with their own individual values, their inner clarity and direction, as a guide to how they might go about improving the quality of their lives. She is now pursuing a new career as a writer and divides her time between France and California.

Introduction

SUPERLIFE: The 7 Steps that Spell S.U.C.C.E.S.S. is a process that will lead you to experience your life in a more fulfilling way.

It is about achieving not only improved material conditions and tangible goals in the world, but also, and perhaps more importantly, the quality of inner well-being and peace of mind that comes entirely within the domain of your own influence and control.

Few of us have the capability to be a superman or a superwoman in the eyes of the world. We do, however, have the ability to achieve a superlife, however we choose to define that. Whether you are a teenager or a senior citizen, a housewife or a corporate executive, you can determine and achieve fulfilment for yourself.

Before you can effect improvements in your life, you need to clarify what you most want. Then, knowing what paths you wish to pursue, you must be willing to take the necessary active steps to bring about your chosen outcomes.

Each chapter offers exercises, some of which may be more relevant for you than others. Some involve paper and pen; some take you actively into the world and others are guided visualizations. You may wish to pre-record on cassette the visualizations so that you can relax and gain a better intuitive understanding of your motivations. All the exercises are designed to assist you to discover and know clearly what you want, and to gain the confidence to achieve it.

Be gentle with yourself as you do the exercises. The passion you have for your life's objectives, and the loving kindness you extend towards yourself, will combine to open you to the ways and means by which you can achieve the quality of life you now want. With a clear vision of your aims in life, the resources, both inner and outer, you need in order to progress, will be attracted to you.

Treat the book as a companion and friend to give you guidance and a helping hand towards your aims and vision. There may be new ideas for you to contemplate and you might have fun experimenting with the exercises. Allow this book to serve you in any way it can to enrich you, and bring you closer to the **Superlife** of your dreams.

Chapter 1

Set Personal Objectives

The most exciting aspect of setting personal objectives is that of discovering, perhaps for the first time, what matters most to you in life, what your true priorities are and what it is you *really* want out of your life. You can reflect on what you enjoy most, and how you can plan for maximum pleasure and fun.

In setting your personal objectives, it is important both to know very clearly what it is you want, and to have an understanding of the motivations behind your goals. It is getting in touch with, knowing and honouring your personal motivations that will sustain you towards the successful fruition of your most keenly felt ambitions.

From the moment you first drew breath in this world, perhaps even before that, you were subject to influences about living here. These may not all have been influences that contributed towards your successful living in the world. Our primary influences were probably our parents, to whom we looked for direction and guidance. In growing up, we may have attempted to live up to their ideals of success. Later, teachers or other adults may have, consciously or otherwise, contributed to our images of happiness and fulfilment. Now, no matter what influences have governed you in the past, you can choose for yourself the plan and outlook that most satisfies *you*.

A common tendency for humans is to keep looking outside ourselves for inspiration, taking our direction from what we think is a good way to live life, from others who seem fulfilled and successful. We are also subject to those who, through advertisement, demonstrate to us in many glossy and appealing forms how the successful individual or family is supposedly spending their time and money. Very convincing they are too, though seldom matched by our own realities. However attractive things might look from the outside, your personal experience is the one that you can determine and have be the most fun and exciting.

We are presented with many distractions that lead us away from the clear understanding of our source of personal satisfaction. You may be a person for whom life is going along quite happily, but underneath, you have the feeling that you could be having more fun and enjoyment. Or you may be someone who is feeling driven to achieve something worthwhile in your life, but so far that worthwhile purpose has not shown up. Your ambition may have something of a hollow ring to it. Or you could be someone who is immensely successful in worldly terms of career and financial achievement, but there remains within you a certain emptiness. You may even be enjoying great success in all dimensions of your life, but realize that there is always more for you to experience.

In clarifying your objectives, form a rounded picture, where all aspects of your life are brought into a harmonious view. As you explore exercises throughout this book, your aims in life will continue to become clearer, so do not get disheartened if by the end of this chapter you have not arrived at the answers to all the questions posed.

In the course of the following chapters, there are examples and exercises that will assist you to expand into the fullness, or fulfilment, of your life, however you may choose to define it. The theme is always a loving one of 'positive focusing'. That loving approach begins with the view you hold of yourself.

Positive focusing comes about through simply training yourself to view yourself and the experiences of your life from a positive perspective, no matter what. And it is simple. However, many – perhaps most – of us have not been raised in that discipline. When you do begin to practise it, you will notice a measurable increase in the quality of your life.

The urge towards successful living is sometimes counterproductive in that it pressures you with impatience and frustration to act before you are ready. There are of course times when life forces a dramatic turn of events. However, where possible, allow time to effect new directions gradually. In this way, you minimize stress and needless distress. This kind of approach was once described to me as being like the minor adjustment that is made at the very tips of the wings of a large aircraft in flight. The adjustment itself is minor, but steadily, over the passage of time, it effects a major change of direction in a large vehicle, without traumatizing the load being carried. The most profound and lasting change happens in such a way that you can bring all parts of your life into new alignment.

The way this process of adjustment works best is when you are feeling most relaxed and receptive; feeling nurtured, safe, supported and open-minded. In this frame of mind, when you hear information from either outside yourself, or within you, you will know clearly whether it is true for you. In the business of a full day, when you are actively engaged in the world, being bombarded by all kinds of sensation and stimulation, it is hard to know who you really are, far less be true to who you are.

There is therefore great value in taking some time and space out from the concerns of your life for re-evaluation, to see whether what you are doing, and the priorities you are choosing in life, are giving you the greatest possible satisfaction. So before you begin to think about objectives, there are some exercises to assist you in that process of re-evaluation.

Whatever your current situation, you might view your life so far as a rich tapestry of information, knowledge and understanding from which you can now make an assessment. It does not matter whether events were experienced positively, or negatively, at the time. Right now, they are simply part of your personal history and can give you significant pointers as to how you may wish to increase your experience of successful living. There may be some kinds of experience you will wish to enjoy more of; others that might not bear repeating. In either event, that knowledge is well worth having and is part of knowing yourself better.

This first exercise is a form of 'brainstorming'. The questions explore six areas and make up an initial taking stock of who you are now. Not all the questions may be relevant for your particular circumstances. However, the ones that are will catch your attention, even if you do not have the answers for them immediately. Unconsciously, you will begin to work on finding the answers. Then, one day, when you are not thinking about it, having a shower or going for a walk, the answer you need will pop into mind.

Taking Stock

You will need a pen and paper for this exercise. Make a note of each heading, and any answers that come to mind as you read the questions. You might like to leave spaces for more ideas to be written in subsequently. You may even find that answers come in your dreams, or when you first wake up, so you might like to have that paper beside your bed so that you can make notes for yourself, before the day's activities absorb all your attention.

Take stock of your life so far in the following areas:
1. Personal Assets
2. Skills
3. Interests
4. Achievements
5. Values
6. Dreams

1. Personal Assets

In the normal course of life, we do not stop to be aware of all that we have going for us. Assets are often thought

---

about in terms of material wealth alone, but it is really worth measuring our 'wealth' in much broader terms.

What are your personal assets or qualities?
(Sense of humour, compassion, generosity etc.)
Who are your people assets?
(Spouse, parents, children, friends, counsellor etc.)
What are your material assets?
(Clothes, books, car, savings etc.)

2. Skills

Think about this one in some detail. We often take our basic skills for granted. For the purpose of this exercise, include skills like reading, writing, driving, typing, word processing, riding a bicycle and so forth.

What skills did you learn at school and still practise?
What career skills do you have?
What leisure or recreational skills do you use?
What skills have you learnt but not used recently?

3. Interests

These could range from anything for which you devote a keen level of enthusiasm to a mild, passive or distant sense of 'I might pursue this if I had more time/money/inclination.'

What do you enjoy reading about?
What interests did you have at school?
Are there any interests you had to put aside for other priorities in your life?
Are your interests more around people, information or materials?
What about the world has the greatest source of fascination for you?
Which interests do you now pursue actively?

4. Achievements

As with the question on skills, please think about this one in some detail. Many people are only too ready to discount their achievements in favour of their failures, mistakes and blunders. Or alternatively, they recall the major and obvious achievements, but overlook the smaller and often very meaningful accomplishments. These might include assisting a child to become a competent reader; building a greenhouse in the garden; getting a poem published; organizing a sponsored swim for a local charity. Winning first prize and a silver cup for coming first in a backstroke swimming race at the age of 7 might not be perhaps major for you in the final assessment of your life, but it could tell you a lot about you, your capacity for winning and values, having been very meaningful for you at the time.

Which of your achievements has given you greatest pleasure?
Which small success has given you most satisfaction?
Have you most enjoyed achieving results on your own or with others?
What do you rate as your most significant accomplishment to date?

5. Values

Our values give us possibly the greatest source of self-motivation and so it is really worth gaining knowledge of our personal values, which are not necessarily those we have inherited from our family, community or nation. Values are located in the heart of each individual and are associated with deep caring and self-esteem.

Which people in your life do you care most about?
What in your current lifestyle do you most value?

Are you aware of any spiritual direction in your life?
What would you miss the most if it were taken away from you?
What current condition in the world most touches your sense of caring and concern?
How would you like to be remembered?

6. Dreams

This is the most fun section. The child within us loves to play, given the permission. I wonder how many of us have submitted the child within to the stern business of earning a living or conforming to an acceptable norm or entering a harsh, time-consuming discipline in order to qualify for some respectable entry into society. So now ask yourself:

If you could do, be or have anything you wanted in the world . . .
. . . what would that be?
What were your fondest dreams as a small child?
What is the one adventure you would most like to have in your life?
If you could create it for yourself, what would be your happiest moment?
What vision brings the greatest feeling of joy in you?
What is your idea of bliss?
What games did you most enjoy playing as a child?

The events and experiences which had greatest intensity for you will register special meaning by catching your attention. The process of brainstorming with questions is a very effective way of bringing knowledge and information to the surface. A building science professor in the architectural department of a university once commented that in any creative or problem-solving situation, the most important beginning was knowing which questions to ask. If you would like to explore any of the sections above in more detail for yourself, you might like to experiment with this approach. Remember to keep all the questions positive and open. In other words, questions that lead only to the answer 'yes' or 'no' will have less value.

Sowing Seeds with Questions

Take a pad of paper and write at the head of the top sheet:
What Are the Most Important Questions to Ask?
Then, allow the questions to pop into mind. The process of asking yourself questions is rather like sowing seeds. Your mind, unconsciously, cannot help but get to work on them. You can leave the questions to 'incubate' until intuitively, you know the answers and the actions you wish to take, if any. Once the questions are out on paper, let them be. Forget about them and do not worry about the answers. The example below shows how this exercise can look.

Concerning my **Values**,
What Are the Most Important Questions to Ask?

- What are the values that have the most meaning for me?
- What were my values growing up?
- How do my values differ now from when I was 15?
- What do I value about my current job?
- How do I value my co-workers?
- Could I get greater satisfaction in another career?
- Do I show that I really value myself?
- How can I best fulfil my spiritual path as well as all my other commitments?
- How does my current lifestyle reflect my values?

- Are there any changes I would like to make in my life in order to honour my values more fully?
- How could I give more time to the people I love and care for most?
- What can I do now to fulfil my values more completely?

This exercise is one that you can apply in many different circumstances. Any time you are feeling stuck and think you do not know how to proceed, experiment with this technique. You may be surprised by the extent of information and understanding you have within you, just for the asking and the willingness to listen patiently for the answers.

Remember that we have one mouth and two ears: you might benefit from listening twice as much as you question. The question mark itself reminds us of the shape of the ear. So once having asked the question, remember to listen.

'Listening' is primarily a matter of being open and receptive. The answers can appear in many forms and from many directions. You may overhear a conversation in a restaurant; read a headline in a newspaper; catch a small but relevant part of a TV report; be walking the dog, and catch yourself thinking something 'out of the blue'.

Your intuitive leads, or 'hunches', could become a great resource for you. Learning to respond to your inner guidance, not blindly, but with careful checking, will awaken you to a new, lighter meaning of the word 'responsible'; that of your ability to respond to life's opportunities. Responsibility becomes a burden when you blame and punish yourself when events turn out less than well. The 'ability to respond', however, is enhanced when your attitude is a relaxed one of forgiveness, compassion and learning, no matter what the outcome. Fault-finding and destructive criticism in yourself and others impedes progress. Open-minded observation and re-evaluation supports your forward movement.

This next exercise is another form of surfacing information from your unconscious resources. The unconscious communicates to us in symbol form. This time you will be drawing, not writing words. No one else need see what you 'draw', nor do you need to be a great artist to benefit from the exercise. It would be good to allow yourself at least 15 minutes to complete all the sections. Sometimes it takes a few minutes for the pictures to surface, so be patient with yourself.

The example in Figure 1 demonstrates how this can look.

Pictorial Diagrams –
Past, Present and Future

Take a sheet of paper, which could be a standard letter size, or larger if you prefer. Divide it into three sections. If you like drawing on a large scale, take three separate sheets of paper. One section will be headed:

Meaningful Life Events and Experiences from the Past

These could be either 'positive' or 'negative', whatever has had an impact on you up until now.

The next section will be headed:

The Person I Am Now

You may include here, in symbol form, whatever is important to you and your life today.

The final section will be headed:

What I Want in the Future

This could include both material gains, and qualities of life, represented in symbol form.

In each section, using no letters, words or numbers, draw symbols that represent answers to the statements in each section. Allow the questioning and critical mind to stand to one side for this exercise and let the images come freely forward.

Figure 1: Past, Present and Future

The symbols in the example represent the following:

Past: Meaningful events and experiences were getting married; a spell in hospital as a child; achieving my pilot's licence; the arrival of our first child; my favourite dog when I was growing up; holidays we used to spend in Cornwall.

Present: Things that are important to me now are my rose garden; my computer; playing tennis and the friends we know at the tennis club; meditation and peacefulness; my home and family.

Future: What I would like in the future is a prize for one of my roses; to expand and sell off our transportation business; to have a relaxed and sunny disposition, and also to visit the South Pacific; to have my first novel published.

This exercise will similarly reveal information about who you are and the key influences and values that you hold. Having drawn out the symbols, you might like to put into words what they mean for you, by writing or talking them through with someone else. What did you learn from doing the exercise? Of all the experiences and thoughts you have had, it might be surprising to observe those that popped into mind over and above all the others.

In an exercise like the last one where you are assessing, or evaluating, your life to date a key word to have in mind is **value.** It is important to regard every event and experience of your life in the light of your gains and benefits. You may have recalled an unhappy experience from your early life, but that could have considerable value for you as an indicator of a motivation in your life.

Before you can make a plan for successful living for yourself, it will help you to consider just what 'success' is. Look beyond a superficial definition of success to the deeper meaning that success has for you. As with the other exercises, allow yourself some time and space to explore the full extent of your personal view of success. This is an important step towards clarifying the objectives that are personal and true for you.

What Is Success for You?

This need not take very long, but do allow yourself to reflect as much as you need, until you have emptied all your thoughts on the subject.

This is a pen and paper exercise and the question at the head of the paper is:

What Does Success Mean for Me?

Divide the paper in half vertically with one half headed 'INNER', and the other 'OUTER'. Allow thoughts about success to surface. Some may have to do with your quality of life; others with material benefit. Some may come under the heading of both 'inner' and 'outer'.

The example below shows how this exercise might begin to look.

WHAT DOES SUCCESS MEAN FOR ME?

Inner
Peace of mind
Self-confidence

Outer
Holiday in the sun
A sports car

Loving friendships

Job satisfaction

Freedom to work the
hours of my choice

A Ph.D. in philosophy

A happy marriage

Physical fitness

As you explore the previous exercises, you may begin to identify the four sides of the square of a fulfilling life. These sides are:

1. Health
2. Wealth
3. Happiness
4. Perfect Self-Expression

1. **Health** includes not just physical, but also mental, emotional and spiritual health.

2. **Wealth** concerns the material well-being that relates to our needs, which is not necessarily the luxury we sometimes associate with the word 'wealth'. This word might be better written as 'wellth'.

3. **Happiness** refers to the loving we experience in our lives, the loving we give and receive with ourselves and others.

4. **Perfect Self-Expression** has to do with our vocation in life. This goes beyond the career at which we work to gain an income, although if you are fortunate, your career will be in alignment with your vocation.

What if true success were a matter of feeling happy, healthy and complete in yourself, able to live confidently within your world? What if success was a quality of freedom and enjoyment in life?

If you have not already done so, you might like to find what is your true vocation in life: that form of self-expression that brings you greatest reward. A vocation is not necessarily constant over the full span of a lifetime. You may enjoy a variety of different forms of expression, from administering an organization, to raising children, to carving woodwork, to promoting a local cause.

Here is an idea you might like to consider:

First find what you most enjoy doing, what unleashes the most creative forces from within you; then, if you need, let people pay you to do it.

This suggestion may not match your current idea of what is practically feasible. You may have financial commitments and obligations that would inhibit you from giving up your accountancy career for the precarious world of stage management, for example.

However, you might like to nurture this idea, like another

seed, in the back of your mind. You never know how circumstances over the coming months and years may move in your favour. People have an inclination to move in the direction of their deepest motives, once they are conscious of them, and find life most rewarding when they do. Often, life experience has deadened us (if temporarily) to the spark of vitality and creativity that awakens us to our greatest potential for fulfilment. Now may be the time for you to pursue the freedom to honour your personal motivations, in consultation with, and consideration of, those who may be affected by your decisions.

You may be at a stage in life where you really have a clean slate as far as creating your future is concerned. You may have just graduated from college and have no dependents or major financial commitments. Alternatively, you may now be able to enjoy the freedom of not having to work for an income, and no longer have the obligations associated with bringing up a family and paying a mortgage.

There are two primary personal benefits that a working career generally offers, apart from the obvious financial income. These are:

1. An occupation or activity that fills a large part of the working day.

2. The companionship of others.

When you are planning your life, you can take into account at the same time the two areas of vocation and the people with whom you would enjoy working and spending your time. Figure 2 is a chart to assist you in taking both areas into account.

The Activity/People Planner provides a framework concerning what you want to do, and those with whom you do it.

The three areas of activity are broadly:

1. Primary occupation or vocation

2. Education or personal development

3. Leisure and recreation

The possibility for companionship ranges from the closest with your spouse, life partner or family members to casual contact with co-workers or members of a social club.

The three options concerning companionship are:

1. Alone
2. With close family/friends
3. Casual friends or acquaintances

The Activity/People Planner will assist you to assess all your needs and priorities concerning the people who are important to you, alongside the activities you wish to undertake. For example, if you are pursuing a correspondence course on your own, you may wish to include other pursuits where you get out and meet others.

If you find that all your activities are with your spouse, you may wish to give one another space to pursue other interests which are enriching for your partnership together. If you are building a small business, remember to make time for the family that you love. Or if you are intensely studying for a qualification, you may benefit greatly from having a refreshing leisure pursuit that is not too time-consuming.

	1 ALONE	2 WITH PARTNER/ FAMILY/CLOSE FRIENDS	3 CASUAL CONTACT
1 OCCUPATION			
2 EDUCATION			
3 LEISURE/ RECREATION			

Figure 2: The Activity/People Planner

There may be some overlap for you in these sections. However, this is simply a guide so that you can aim for a happy balance in your life.

If you are in the position of having a clean slate for planning your life ahead, you are well placed for discovering and living in alignment with your Personal Motivational Trend. This may not be the case for you if you are currently fully committed in a career with financial obligations. The good news, in that case, is that you have possibly greater leeway in effecting the adjustments you might want in the future. Time can serve you in this way.

A Personal Motivational Trend has to do with three main factors:

1. Enjoyment
2. Achievement
3. Your Experience of Success

During the course of your life so far, you will have enjoyed a number of successes, not necessarily great judged by the world, but meaningful in the context of your own life as you view it. You will have discovered certain kinds of skills you enjoy using, like cooking, communicating, working with figures, selling. You will also know the environments in which you thrive the best. There may be many factors that contribute to your enjoyment, achievement and experience of success, and these may now be hidden from your conscious attention.

This next exercise is another for bringing forward knowledge and understanding that you have within you, in a specific and positively-focused way. This is the first of the guided visualization exercises mentioned in the Introduction. Remember you will need some time to yourself, in which you will not be disturbed. You may wish to record the visualization on tape so that you can close your eyes and listen without any outer visual distractions. Alternatively, you may wish to do the exercises in stages. After you read each paragraph, close your eyes as you visualize and reflect on it. With a pen and paper, make notes as you go. However, as before, ensure that the time you take is undisturbed by any outside distractions so that you can listen inwardly as fully as possible. Before you begin this exercise, have a pen and paper or notebook handy so that you can make any notes you would like afterwards.

Your Personal Motivational Trend

You could either do this exercise looking at your life as a whole up to now; alternatively, repeat the process for chunks of time of say 5 years, or 10 years. So you would do the exercise first from the age of 0 to 5, or 10; then from 6 to 10, or 11 to 20; then from 11 to 15, or 21 to 30, and so on.

Sit in a place in which you can be relaxed, but one in which you will stay awake and not fall asleep. Begin by taking in a few deep breaths.

As you breathe in deeply . . . breathe in a deeper relaxation . . . and as you breathe out . . . let go of any tensions or distractions . . . observe your breathing . . . and if any thoughts or feelings surface . . . watch them and let them go . . . like clouds passing over a clear blue sky . . . breathe in and expand the peaceful quality within you . . .

Bring to mind an event . . . an occasion in which you experienced success . . . an event in which you demonstrated a skill . . . quality . . . or ability . . . what was it you did? . . . re-live that action now . . . notice if there was anyone else with you . . . or were you alone? . . . did you receive any acknowledgement . . . from yourself . . . or others? . . . was there any prize or award associated with your success? . . . what were the personal assets or qualities you demonstrated? . . . perseverance? . . . humour? . . . discipline? . . . wisdom? . . . where did you accomplish your success? . . . were you indoors . . . or outside . . . what is the nature of the environment around you? . . . notice all the details of this experience . . . the temperature . . . any particular colours . . . textures . . . or forms . . . that catch your attention now . . .

What was so enjoyable for you about achieving this success? . . . what was especially fun for you? . . . what gives you the greatest feeling of enthusiasm? . . . Breathe deeply now into that feeling of enthusiasm . . . and expand it within you . . .

Let the quality of vitality and enthusiasm bubble through the whole of your body . . . feel yourself coming alive . . . increasing your personal store of enjoyment . . . pleasure . . . and fulfilment . . .

Maintain those good feelings within you as you now . . . very gently . . . and in your own timing . . . become aware of where you are now . . . and open your eyes . . .

Make a note on paper of any key phrases, or insights that you gained about your Personal Motivational Trend. Particularly notice the action(s) you were taking and the Experience of Success/Enjoyment as you progressed towards a successful end result.

For example, you may have discovered how much you enjoy your creative ability in baking cakes for weddings and birthdays; that you have a talent for combining textures and flavours and colours; that you have an intuitive sense of timing for your cakes; that you enjoy the artistic flair of creating a specially designed cake for each client; that you appreciate the acknowledgement and referrals given to you by your clients.

It is well worth exploring this exercise for more than one period of your life, enjoyable too, bringing back to mind moments when you experienced yourself at your best. The purpose is to identify the various different strands that go towards making up your unique grain.

The following exercise, this time with paper and pen, may further assist you in discovering more about your Personal Motivational Trend.

What I Love(d) About . . .

Cast your mind over your life so far and focus on one event or experience that was in any way a high point for you. It could have been at work, or at school, or something you did just for the fun of it.

In a few words, write down this event as a heading.

Now, answer any of the following questions that may be relevant to your heading:

- What was it about this event or experience that was so special for you?
- Were you actively involved in some way, or more of an observer?
- What was the most delightful moment that you can recall within the event or experience?
- Were there any special insights you received, about yourself, or the world as a whole?
- How would you describe the most dominant positive quality that you experienced?
- What did this event or experience tell you about yourself?
- Is there anything else you would like to note down?

The information you gain from these exercises will give you a pattern of self-knowledge that will act as a guide for setting the objectives that will give you both the experience of success, and enjoyment on the way to achieving them.

Below are some examples of people who used their awareness of their Personal Motivational Trends to plan their lives.

- One woman at a seminar had recently lost her job through the relocation of her company. Her loves in life were brass band music, typing and animals. She resolved to find typing work in an environment concerned with animals. It was suggested to her that she might apply to a local zoo, which was also in close proximity of brass band music at lunchtimes.

- A successful architect in his 50s sold his practice and while he had no need to produce more income, nevertheless enjoyed the business of making property deals. He still had the love of buildings, which he had had as a young man working on building sites, long before he studied architecture. The smell and feel of timber, bricks and mortar continued to have a particular appeal for him. In addition, he had developed more recently a keen interest in alternative healing methods. He combined these interests by becoming involved in the development of healing centres.
- The wife of an early-retiring bank manager had always wanted to train to become a nurse. In her 50s, she did not want to train for qualifications, but recognized that what had motivated her towards nursing was the care of people within a hospital community. While her husband took up a new part-time career, she volunteered her time at a local nursing home where she could fulfil that original motivational trend.
- A young man who was highly numerate, and had great pleasure in the business of handling money, trained in book-keeping. As much as he enjoyed working with figures, he did not like being inside a city office for the whole of his working day. He happily gave up his office job to become a bus conductor, still handling money but spending his time at least partly out of doors.

  It does take courage sometimes to admit what is fulfilling for you because it may not conform to what others have come to expect of you.
- A couple attending a two-day retirement seminar had heard in the introduction encouragement to pursue their dreams. It was only at the final Open Forum of closing remarks that he admitted that he had a longing to learn gliding; and she said the one thing she had

always wanted to do was go ballooning. They had not dared to disclose their dreams to one another before.

- A young man who went against the wishes of his parents pursued a dream to learn the hotel and catering business in Switzerland. He became very resourceful in financing himself through his training and learning a second language. Although it was not an easy route for him, his character and personality grew with his effort. He finally bought a small but exclusive hotel which has become very popular, and his parents very much enjoy spending the occasional weekend there.

Once you are true to whatever evokes the maximum enthusiasm in your life, your sense of enjoyment and vitality will contribute a sparkle to the lives of others, which will be hard for them to resist. It may be that your circle of friends changes to one in which others more completely match your interests in life.

You may know people in their 80s who radiate this quality of enthusiasm and have a youthfulness that makes them appear much younger than they are. Alternatively, you may also know young people in their teens and 20s who are weighed down with life's concerns and who appear aged with dullness, intensity and pessimism. Personal vitality is not a function of age.

Getting in touch with, and living in alignment with, what motivates you from within will release your greatest resources and increase your pleasure in life. Life for you will be far from dull.

An important human motivator that you might like to consider is that of learning something new. As children, our natural curiosity directed us in our initial learning about our world, and how to conduct ourselves within it. Your sense of curiosity remains with you throughout life. We live in an exciting world where the pace of change always seems to be increasing. There is always more to discover. We have the choice: either to resist the new, or treat the changes as part of an adventure in which we can play a part.

How could you enhance and bring your sense of curiosity more fully into play in your life? Even the wisest and most knowledgeable people admit to how little they really know. It seems as though the more you seem to know, the less you really do know. There is always more. The question to ask is perhaps: what kind of 'more' would you like to know? What area of learning, growth or development would now challenge and stimulate your personal assets and resources?

There may be a new skill that appeals to you, that you would enjoy developing. Is there a fresh field of knowledge that you would now like to explore? There are increasing numbers of people, no longer engaged in full-time work, who are now entering further education courses, not to gain qualifications for a career, but just for the sheer pleasure of learning.

The late teens or the 20s perhaps represents the time when you are embarking on life after your full-time education. However, you could also view yourself as 'embarking on life' in your 40s, 50s or even 60s and 70s. Your life up to that point could be considered your 'education' and now you are ready to enter your life's greatest purpose and achievement. There are some people whose lives were not fulfilled until they were well into their 70s.

Take care that popular opinion about what can be achieved at any age does not condition you to a limited expectation of your capacity for success. Whatever your greatest accomplishment to date, whatever your age, you might now be ready to move into a peak of fulfilment in your life. To take one example, a 12-year-old with a keen vision and enthusiasm for helping the homeless in his city rallied the support of adults and generated the resources he needed to realize his vision.

An exciting life for you may have to do with viewing your contribution in the light of your maximum fulfilment, where there is a quality of expanding into the fullness of your life. You may have already experienced such moments of expansion, such as at the birth of your child; witnessing a sunset; listening to Mozart; an experience of the spiritual light within you. The experience of expansion into the fullness of who you are comes in a relatively fleeting moment, and cannot be grasped and held forever. However, you can direct your life in such a way as to have more of those moments, if you so choose.

You may wish to strike out into a totally new occupation, with mainly your native wit and enthusiasm to guide you. If you are in such a phase of life, then the following words may encourage you:

The *willingness* to do gives the *ability* to do. The resources you need to accomplish your goal will meet you at the point of your action.

The following example is about someone who followed closely his personal motivation and inspiration to embark on a project without initially knowing a lot about how to fulfil it.

The man in question was deeply moved by the dismantling of the Berlin Wall and what that represented for him in terms of the barriers also being dissolved within individuals and between nations. Never having been published before, he resolved to make a book of photographs and quotes that highlighted his vision of a more peaceful world without conflict. With a clarity of purpose and direction, he took hundreds of photographs of the wall in various stages of its coming down, and gathered quotes from many unusual sources.

He decided to by-pass the slower route of publishing houses and found his own printer in Singapore and international distributors. His enthusiasm drew to him the right resources at the right times in surprising and unexpected ways. He was both profoundly motivated by what he was producing, and also learned much about producing and selling books.

Embarking on a completely new venture, learning a new discipline, set of skills, occupation, profession or field of knowledge will pay you great dividends. You have a great deal to gain from attempting a new endeavour. At the very least, you will discover more about what is true for you, more about your priorities and values. It may not even turn out exactly the way you first envisaged. You could find that once you strike out and make a change from your previous routine and expectations, the process of 'serendipity' may take you on yet another path, which is even closer to what you are really wanting.

In order to stimulate some creative thinking in your life, you may need simply to start doing something different; or doing the same things in different ways. This may sound simplistic to you; in a way it is. Do you always go to work by the same route? Take a different one, and see how your perspective changes. You might have fun looking at the routines you have during the week, then making a point of doing everything in another way. Put your left shoe on first, instead of the right. Get up half an hour earlier. Buy a different newspaper. Move the furniture around in your living room. Start looking at life from different angles and notice the changes you experience. If you fail to give yourself the opportunity to explore new paths, you will never know the rewards they might bring you.

The next exercise is another step towards clarifying your personal objectives. It is best done when you are feeling most open and relaxed. Allow your creative imagination to have a free rein and for the purpose of this exercise, allow your rational mind to stand aside. When it comes to making a plan, then you can bring your reasoning into play.

Your Magic Wand

Just for the length of this exercise, imagine that you do have a clean slate in life, with no special commitments or obligations to fulfil. If you could wave a Magic Wand, and you could have anything you wanted in the world, what would you have?

What if you could **do, be** or **have** whatever you wanted in life? Forget that anything may seem out of the question at the moment.

Your Magic Wand is really your Magic Want. Repeat the following questions consecutively at least five times, or more, and answer them either in your mind, or written on paper. Allow the answers to pop into mind spontaneously, and do not censor them, so that you let your stream of consciousness flow freely.

When a thought registers particularly strongly, make a note where you will be able to refer back to it. Have fun and allow your creativity to come into play.

1. What do you want?
2. How can you get it?
3. What is the experience you are looking for?

There are no 'right' or 'wrong' answers to these questions. A want could be as simple as picking a rose, or as grand as your personal, private jet; or an experience of freedom, excitement or peacefulness. You may discover through this exercise that there are many ways of producing what you want, not necessarily practical, but that does not matter here.

As a conclusion to this exercise, list five things you want to have, do or be.

Example:

1. Fly around the world on Concorde
2. Have a prize-winning rose garden
3. Raise £500,000 for the local hospital
4. Be a successful football coach
5. Conduct the Royal Philharmonic Orchestra for one evening

Having explored with the imagination the possibilities that

would most inspire you for the future, we shall now begin to look into the process of planning towards specific aims. Between now and, say, three years' time, many events and much information will come to light that will influence you. However, having objectives for three years ahead will provide a reference point towards which you can align yourself. You may know very clearly that in three years' time you mean to achieve your first degree, if you are embarking upon your university career.

There will be other stages in your life where you will not have a clear idea of specific external goals, but you may know that there are certain inner qualities you will want to be experiencing more of in your life, such as improved communication within your marriage; or, greater satisfaction in your career, whether that is within your existing job, or in a different one; time for more social life with your friends, more excitement, fun and challenge.

Make a plan with major objectives for three years ahead. Then, bringing your attention forward, think about what you will accomplish in the next year towards fulfilling those objectives. The next span of time to consider would be the next six months. This becomes more specific now. What will you achieve by a date six months from now, to bring you closer to your one-year goals, and three-year objectives?

The next spans of time would be three months, one month and one week. If you are well practised in setting goals for yourself, you will probably be very accurate in estimating the time required to accomplish certain objectives. However, know that setting a time limit is an estimation at best. You have not failed if you find that you do need more time to make something happen. There may be factors that appear that you could not have initially anticipated.

In the course of going towards your goals, you may find that you need to make some course adjustments before you arrive at your final aim. The value of objectives and goals is that they do provide a direction into which you can channel your energies, and give you a sense of accomplishment as you progress.

In setting out your objectives, take into account clearly both those which are directly within your sphere of control and influence, and those which will be conditioned by events outside your control. You may find the greatest satisfaction in having a balance of 'inner' and 'outer' objectives.

There are three sections for you to consider:

Section 1
   Health and Fitness
   Personal Philosophy
   Religious/Spiritual
Section 2
   Family
   Home
   Close Relationships
   Community Service
   Leisure/Recreation
Section 3
   Career/Status
   Salary
   Financial/Investment
   Possessions/Holidays/Lifestyle

Section 1 relates most closely to our inner environment and how we experience our lives. This is the area most personal to us and over which we have the greatest control. The inner environment is deeply precious to us, the source of our well-being, personal inspiration and self-motivation. It is also closely associated with maintaining good physical health. There can be no greater gift that we give to ourselves than strengthening our inner worlds, and physically treating ourselves well.

Section 2 also concerns our inner being, but in close relation to the outer world, where we are possibly most vulnerable, exposed, and at the same time, blessed and fulfilled. Curiously, it is an area where we have a very great degree of personal control but not in the way that usually happens in family and social life. This is perhaps the most exciting area of development for us as individuals, being honest with ourselves in the circumstances immediately around us. There is scope in this section for the greatest satisfaction in life.

Finally, Section 3 is the one that in my experience is usually given greatest importance, if not the only significance, in terms of setting objectives in life. Although we are obviously involved and participating in producing results in this area, we are at the same time subject to influences outside of our control.

There is a greater distance between our inner world, in which we exercise a great deal of choice, and the outer world of economic climate, political whim, market trend and popular opinion. However, strength and personal alignment in Sections 1 and 2 greatly enhance our capacity for achievement in this Section.

Your Ideal Scene

This exercise is a guided visualization in which you may wish to put to one side the practical, rational side of your mind to allow your imagination plenty of scope. Have a notebook or journal by your side so that you can make any notes you would like after it.

You will be exploring an ideal day three years away from today's date in which you will experience yourself living successfully in all aspects of your life: your all-round health; your relationships at home, with friends and colleagues; your vocation or career, holidays, home; any form of self-expression that is important to you. This will be a time in which you experience increased vitality within and around yourself, confidence, enjoyment; where both you and your world appreciate and value you for who you are.

As before, relax yourself fully . . . Make sure you will be undisturbed . . . . Sit comfortably where you will stay awake and aware . . .

Breathe in deeply . . . let that breath out and let go of any tensions . . . mental . . . physical . . . emotional . . . spiritual

. . . *Take in another deep breath . . . and breathe in relaxation*
. . . breathe out . . . and be aware of a peacefulness within you
. . .

With your eyes closed . . . become more aware of your inner
worlds . . . the strengths . . . and qualities that are vibrantly
alive within you . . . You know what they are . . . now you
can have time to know them better . . . to view them actively
contributing towards the fulfilment of your life . . .

Bring your attention forward now to a point of time . . . three
years from now . . . The date will be . . . Feel . . . see . . . hear
. . . yourself on this ideal day . . . Everything is going your
way . . . the conditions around you support you fully in your
deepest ambitions . . . What are the conditions around you?
. . . Where are you? . . . Who is with you? . . . Or are you
alone? . . . How do you look? . . . How are you dressed? . . .
Is there anything about your health and fitness that you notice?
. . . What is the greatest achievement you notice in your life
now? . . .

How do you feel about yourself on this ideal day? . . . What
qualities do you experience yourself demonstrating fully now?
. . . Which of your strengths are you most aware of? . . . What
activities are giving you greatest satisfaction? . . . What is it
about you and your world now that is giving you most
fulfilment? . . .

What do you notice about the people you love and care for?
. . . How are you spending time with your friends? . . . How
do you spend your free time? . . . How are you having fun? . . .

How is your life at work . . . in your daily occupation . . .
studies? . . . . . How are you demonstrating your success in this
area of your life? . . . How are you fulfilling your personal
mission? . . . How do you view yourself in the light of your
ideals? . . . How are you honouring your deepest motivations?
. . .

What is giving you the greatest feeling of enthusiasm now?
. . . Is it something you are doing? . . . Is it someone you are
with? . . . What is your happiest moment on this ideal day?

> . . . *If there were one word, one quality, to describe yourself now . . . what would it be? . . .*
>
> *See that quality written in large letters in front of you . . . Hear it being sung within you . . . Feel that quality radiating through you so fully . . . that it extends in waves to the world around you . . .*
>
> *Staying in touch with that quality . . . very gently and gradually . . . bring your attention back to this present moment . . . to your room and where you are now sitting . . .*
>
> *While the images are still fresh in your mind, make any notes that you would like so that you have as a reference your ideal scene as you imagined it.*

Now, having used your imagination to create an Ideal Scene for yourself in three years' time, we will now look at bringing that vision into a reality. This next stage requires practical thinking about the steps you will take, the action that is necessary, to make it all happen. Your Ideal Scene can serve to inspire and enthuse you. However, take care that in the practical planning you do not set yourself too tough a programme. Have it be as much fun as possible for yourself. The plan is set out as follows:

1. Final Objectives
2. Interim Goals
3. Immediate Targets

The following chart is a guide for you to note your objectives and an outline of the goals and targets that are steps towards achieving those objectives.

The overall plan gives you a guide for both the objective and goals, and time scales. In practice, you will probably find it more effective to have two separate pages for each of the three sections. The first page covers the broader plan (three years to six months) and the second, the more immediate and detailed goals and targets.

CONTENTS OF YOUR PERSONAL 3-YEAR PLAN

Section 1	**Section 2**	**Section 3**
Health/Fitness	Family/Home	Career/Status
Philosophy	Friends/Colleagues	Salary/Income
Spiritual/	Community Service	Investments
Religious	Leisure/Recreation	House/Holidays/
		Car/etc

3 year
OBJECTIVES

1 year
GOALS

6 month
GOALS

3 month
GOALS

1 month
TARGETS

1 week
TARGETS

Example from Section 1:

In the area of your health, perhaps you would like to achieve a bodyweight of 130 pounds (59 kg/9 st 4). You are currently 165 pounds (75 kg/11 st 11) and have already attempted a number of diets with spasmodic success. The weight has always gone back after the initial good intentions. As a three-year objective, you would write in 130 lb. Recognizing that this is an area in which you have yet to prove yourself successful, what would be a realistic goal for one year ahead? Say 155 lb (70 kg/11 st 1).

An approach that unconsciously defeats dieters is the sense of loss in respect of not eating favourite (and fattening) foods. Similarly, aiming for too much too soon discourages and defeats the best of intentions. It is better to aim positively for

1. The preferred bodyweight
2. Eating habits that nourish your body

That positive orientation will lead to greater success. Underpinning this is of course a genuine want for the change. Knowing how the new bodyweight will come into line with a personal mission will bring in an extra inspiration and enthusiasm for meeting the challenges.

A six-month goal might be to have identified the combinations of foods that best nurture your particular body. Some bodies function better with more carbohydrate and less protein, for example. Most gain weight with fats and sugars. You may find that as you begin the process of exploring constructively your eating habits, you are drawn towards the resources that can assist you.

Your more immediate targets might include going to the library to find your first book on good nutrition.

In the process of getting what you want, you may find that you achieve your three-year objective within, say, 18 months. However, having the objective further away does allow you to fluctuate in weight in that time, without experiencing 'defeat'. Part of your task now may include healing the memory of all those times when you did not succeed in achieving all that you wanted.

Example from Section 2:

A personal ambition might be having your first novel accepted for publication in three years' time. In one year's time, you could have had a short story accepted for publication, the concept for your novel having taken some shape with some scenes and characters already sketched out. In the next six months, you will have established a routine within your daily life for sitting down and writing and have knowledge of your pace and speed of creative writing.

Within three months, you might have set up for yourself a mentor, supportive writing group or others with whom you can exchange knowledge and ideas about creative writing. In the next month, you could write your first short story. In the next week, let your family know what you are planning to do so that you have their support and co-operation for the time you will be spending in the spare room, potting shed or attic at your typewriter or word processor.

Example from Section 3:

A three-year career objective could be to set up your own professional practice as an accountant. In one year's time, you will have the beginnings of your own client list. In six months, there will be those in your community who know of your plans and you will have your first part-time client.

In three months, you will have a clear strategy for setting up the practice, and a room at home from which to work in your spare time. In one month, you will be familiar with all the steps you will need to take, legally and otherwise, in order to practise independently. You will also know whether you would like to go into partnership with another accountant. In the next week, you will discuss your thoughts with your family and let them know as far as you are able how your plan might affect them.

The value of setting out your plans clearly is that they can be reviewed: the weekly ones, weekly; monthly ones, monthly; and so on. At each stage, you can monitor and check that the steps you have set out are the most appropriate. Constant updating in this way will keep you in touch with what you want, and moving steadily in the direction you want to go.

A technical example of this idea is that of a jet which is set on automatic pilot to go from, say, London to Los Angeles. If you were to look at the flight path, it would not be a straight line. Factors such as turbulent air currents will cause the aircraft to go 'off course' periodically. So it is constantly being brought back 'on course' for its destination. Similarly, you may find yourself making course adjustments as you progress towards your target.

The plans you make may also serve as a record of your progress and so you may wish to retain them. There is often nothing very complicated in setting about achieving what you want. Knowing clearly enough what you want may be the most difficult aspect of achieving fulfilment. The steps to getting there are a matter of taking action over a period of time. The greatest obstacles are probably within you and we will be addressing those, and how to overcome them, in the following chapters.

Possibly the primary value of setting objectives is that they give you a route to go from A (now) to B (then). Choosing your Bs is what setting objectives is all about. Then living successfully is not only about what you achieve at point B, but importantly, inwardly, on the way there, discovering who you are more fully, and revealing the resources you bring into play that make you both unique and very much a integral part of your world.

If you were to look at any of the products of our hi-tech environment, you might marvel at the design and ingenuity of them. However, it is not until they are put in motion and functioning that the magnificence of contemporary inventions can be fully appreciated. However extraordinary are the products of human invention, they fall a long way short of the immense potential energy and resource of human output. When you are ready to expand into the fullness of who you are, then you may begin to discover the fun, excitement and exhilaration of living successfully.

The next chapters will assist you in the process of further clarifying what you want; then taking the simplest, most enjoyable steps towards the fulfilment of your goals. With each achievement, you will increase the value you hold of yourself and you will continue to evolve a clearer understanding of exactly what your main objectives in life are. As a part of this process, you will find your plans changing accordingly.

Your individual plan can be any form that is most clear for you. The framework suggested here can be improvised, put into diagram form, sketched as a chart or made so that it is both appealing and fun for you, as much as it is clear. Your individual plan, incorporating both your three-year objective overview, and some of the more detailed goal steps, can be in any form you like – whatever is most clear to you.

A final exercise concerning your objectives is that of formulating a Personal Mission Statement. You may not be ready to do this until you have read subsequent chapters, so feel free to return to it later. The processes of Unlocking Your Attitude, Clearing Away Blocks, Creating Inner Strength, Expecting Success and Simply Having Fun will lead you into a heightened perception of yourself, from which you can experience a much greater vision for yourself. This vision will contain all the elements that make up a fulfilling life for you. It is likely to embrace something of your personal philosophy and spiritual motivation.

When you have your vision in mind, stated simply in a sentence or short paragraph, you will have a set of guidelines within which you can align yourself and your objectives.

Your Personal Mission Statement

Allow yourself plenty of time and space to reflect on the following:

What values have the most meaning for you?
What are your greatest talents?
How would you most like to serve others?
What is your vocation now?
What is your greatest personal asset?
What does loving mean for you, in daily practice?

In forming your Personal Mission Statement, you are not aiming to fulfil it perfectly in each moment. It is there as a guide, something to re-focus on from time to time, to re-inspire you and give you confidence to lift above your challenges as you move forward.

Once you have your Personal Mission Statement, you might like to write it somewhere so that you can easily refer to it from time to time. You might like to read it through first thing in the day, or last thing at night for a good night's sleep, or at those times when you are most open, relaxed and receptive.

Examples

- The quality of my teaching serves my students in the fulfilment of their dreams and ambitions.
- My home and family are flourishing through my loving, sensitivity and wisdom as a wife and mother.
- As a perceptive and articulate communicator, I am inspiring my readers and viewers in a vision of individual and world peace.
- My gifts of enthusiasm serve to encourage and stimulate increased vitality in our community.

You may feel inclined to have a Personal Mission Statement relating to more than one area of your life. For now, however, select simply one that reflects your greatest personal values and has the maximum emotive appeal for you. Your Statement will have a strong motivational quality as it reflects to you the inner alignment of your personal resources and talents as you bring them to serve your values and deepest aspirations.

Your experience of success in life will be enhanced through fusing your Three-Year Plan with your Personal Mission Statement. As you progress through life, both your objectives and mission in life may evolve and change with each experience of success. A younger person starting out in life will naturally have a very different set of values and objectives from someone in their 90s. What is important is that no matter at what stage you find yourself now, you appreciate your value and you do whatever it takes to enjoy your life to the full.

Chapter 2

Unlock Your Attitude

One of the first lessons to learn about successful living is:

How you view what happens to you contributes towards the quality of success you experience in life. In other words, successful living has a lot to do with the attitude you adopt.

If we were to look, for example, at the world of insurance selling, we might find a career where maintaining a positive attitude and focus towards a goal was not only hard, but also necessary for survival. The insurance sales agent is almost guaranteed many rejections before gaining a positive response. He or she needs to pay constant attention to building up inner reserves of confidence.

It would be much easier to give up in discouragement just before making the essential next call that will lead to a sale. The temptation to giving up further effort could lead to feelings of personal 'failure'. In the longer term, however, those seemingly 'non-productive' steps taken could each contribute information as to how to improve an approach or presentation. In which case, not only was nothing lost, but it might be possible to count many gains for each interaction.

You have probably heard that, generally speaking, having a 'positive attitude' in life is desirable. There is a direct link between what you consider to be a 'positive attitude', and your personal philosophy, which embraces your values and the qualities that best sustain your well-being in life. Exploring

your personal philosophy will not only bring you closer to
clarifying your Personal Mission Statement, mentioned in *Set
Personal Objectives,* but also in establishing objectives for your
inner life.

If you are working within a strong corporate or professional
culture, be aware that your view and philosophy of life will be
moulded by that structure, and similarly other outer
environments. These influences could be to the detriment of
you as an individual because they may take away from your
personal strengths and convictions about life. While it is
valuable and necessary to live within the parameters of a
company structure (if you are in one) or professional conduct –
legal, accountancy, architectural, teaching etc. – it is also
important that you know, and are true to, your self and your
innermost aspirations. These may be different.

Learning about choosing rewarding occupations, personal
values, fulfilling relationships and managing change are areas
of education from which we could all benefit at any age or
stage of our lives.

This next exercise will assist you in clarifying the positive
approaches towards life that best sustain you. It is one that you
might like to reflect over more than one sitting as you may find
that ideas come to mind over a period of time. Knowing the
state of mind that best maintains for you an optimum view of
life is like having a personal guiding light that can keep you
on course with your objectives.

Positive Attitude –
What Is It For Me?

For this exercise, take a pad of paper and pen, write the
following question at the top of the page and jot down
your answers:

What does Positive Attitude or Positive State of Mind mean for me?

Take some time with this exercise, and let the ideas pop into your mind. Listen for ideas when other people are talking, or when you read or listen to the radio or TV. Start noticing, and making a note of, Positive Attitudes or Positive States of Mind at home, work and the world around you. When you find them, add them to your list, if they are in any way true for you.

For example:

> Optimism
> Getting on with things
> Smiling
> Looking on the bright side
> Taking some exercise every day
> Being decisive

As a conclusion to the exercise, you might like to have a page in your notebook or journal headed: 'My Personal Philosophy . . .' and a sentence or paragraph that would summarize it for you. Your Personal Philosophy will have a positive orientation and be sustaining for you as a set of guidelines for your life. Notice how it relates now to your Personal Mission Statement.

For example:

> My personal philosophy is:
>> to be sensitive towards and appreciate others' views and needs
>> to look for the positive benefits that are often hidden in difficult situations
>> that when I am able to love others unconditionally, with no strings attached, the loving gets returned to me in ways and at times I never expect.

Once you have identified more about your personal philosophy as it relates to a positive state of mind, 'lean into' the ways you can incorporate it more fully into your life, not as a punishing routine but with a light touch, as if you were adjusting the finest hi-tech equipment, or making pastry by hand.

There is a danger that having a positive attitude can become fraught with limiting rules, shoulds, oughts, musts and have-tos, which become pressures that block the happy flow of life. Perhaps we all know that we should have a positive attitude, but what about those times when we feel less than positive? It is after all a rich part of our human nature to experience a wide range of feelings and emotions.

Sometimes we try to live up to an image or expectation of ourselves as perfectly accommodating in all circumstances. Put like that it does look a little ridiculous. More serious, though, is the damage we do to ourselves by inflicting too high and too inhuman expectations on ourselves, when we admonish ourselves with a *should*, such as:

- I should have been more considerate towards my employees
- I should have done better in my career
- I should have been kinder to my mother-in-law
- I should feel happier about doing the housework
- I should have done a better deal
- I should have saved more money while I was employed
- I should be looking forward to going to the party

We hold ourselves down by the shoulders. 'Shoulder' has in it the word *should*. The *shoulds* that we put upon ourselves literally create tension in the neck and shoulders. Those pressures can even extend further down the spine and result in various forms of back pain. The *shoulds* that we allow to pressure us squeeze out our vitality and the spontaneous enjoyment of life.

An important move towards your success is reducing as much as you can the redundant, unnecessary pressures that have restricted your positive experience of life in the past.

Do you have any experiences from the past that you have

considered 'failures'? These might be relationships that went 'wrong', exams not passed, getting fired or laid off, not living up to the expectations of others or ourselves, missed opportunities, those millions you could have made if only . . . Such failures from the past may still be within you, limiting now the energy you have available to you because there remains some sense of regret, a sense of 'I could have done better'.

The truth of the matter is that when we look back, it is sometimes easy to see just how we might have done better. However, life is usually fired at us point blank, and we simply do the best we know how at the time. In hindsight, you may discover that the more drastic the 'mistake', the richer the opportunity for gaining greater wisdom and learning. Rather than punishable offences, our mistakes can be viewed as the gifts through which we enrich our lives.

The following exercise will help you to review those disasters, with a fresh look.

Transforming the Failures . . . Into Winning Experiences!

Bring a 'failure' to mind and jot some notes down about it. What happened? Was anyone else involved? Where did it happen? What did you do, or not do, that produced the 'failure'? What was the most disastrous aspect of this event? You can probably write quite a lot of detail about this – we often recall vividly the worst aspects of our tragedies. However, for the purpose of this exercise, an outline sketch will do fine.

Put that to one side, and reflect for a moment on the benefits that you gained from the experience. It might have altered your outlook, or the course of your life in some way, which ultimately was only to your good. Did you develop any special strengths or qualities? Did you learn anything about yourself or others that helped you in some way later on? Was that experience a valuable preparation for an event later in life? The best way to do this exercise is to keep going until you are so full of the benefits of that 'negative' experience, that you come to a point of gratitude for having had it. This may be a tall order for you. However, do your best to keep an open mind towards it and allow that one day in the future, you will fully discover the blessings that happened to arrive in that particular disguise.

When you have transformed your 'failures' into 'successes', and yourself into the attitude of gratitude, you are well on your way to 'unlocking your attitude'.

The following example demonstrates this exercise:

Failure – Being Fired From a Managerial Job

I knew deep down it was coming. There was another manager who seemed to be sabotaging my efforts and pointing out my faults to the boss behind my back. I was having some troubles at home at the same time, which I carried into my work. The baby was teething, and neither my wife nor I were sleeping very well. I got isolated from the group that was making the decisions. I did not stand full enough in support of my own convictions. Our teenager was found stealing money from my wife's purse. I did not really like the nature of the business we were engaged in. My heart was neither in my job, nor the product we were marketing.

The Benefits

1. I was saved having to give in my resignation.
2. I had the benefit of redundancy payment.
3. I learnt that I need to spend more 'quality' time with my wife and family so that they have more of my loving and support.
4. I was glad to be out of an environment that I did not like very much.
5. I learnt that the kind of work that suits me best is more oriented towards research, and less towards managing people.
6. During my period of unemployment, I was able to sleep in shifts with my wife, so that we could take it in turns to comfort the baby.
7. I had some time and space to re-think where I wanted to go with my career.
8. I took time to take our teenager to a counsellor and find out what was disturbing him. He is now happier and we have got closer.
9. I enjoy better communications with my current work colleagues.
10. Through that experience, I learnt more about myself and I am now truer to my personal values.
11. If it had not been for being fired, I would not now have the job I enjoy so much.
12. I am very grateful for all that experience taught me. I will take my former boss out for a drink and let him know how much I appreciated the sensitive way he supported me in leaving that company.

You may have easily recognized the idea of attitude as being a state of mind, or set of beliefs about life. You may also have recognized yourself, or others around you, as having a rigid attitude in certain situations. We can become very set in our ways with an inflexible set of beliefs about the way life is, and this can limit our scope for expansion into a more successful lifestyle.

What if our attitudes and actions have a very direct bearing on the inner and outer quality of our lives? Then, up to now, however we have approached life and what we have been doing has given us the experiences and material results that we have achieved so far. Now, if we wish to improve the quality of our lives, both materially and otherwise, we may need to change not only what we do, but also how we approach doing it. In the process of change, perhaps the first and most challenging task is to effect the necessary change of attitude.

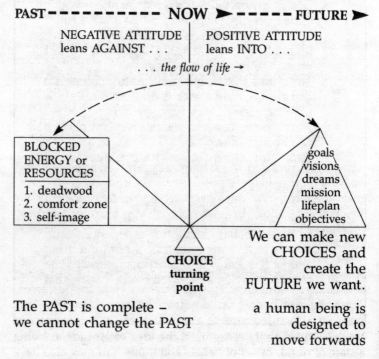

Figure 3: The Choice/Attitude Model

In this chapter, we will be discovering how we always have the inherent power to choose the attitude or state of mind that will best sustain us towards the successful achievement of our objectives. In fact, making wise choices of attitude is in itself very empowering.

Here we come to a second definition of 'attitude'.

Attitude is the direction we lean, or move, in life.

In order to transform your attitude, you simply need to change the direction in which you lean or move. This is easily stated but is not necessarily mastered overnight. Exercises in future chapters are designed to assist you to move more easily in the direction of your choice.

The Choice/Attitude Model (Figure 3) illustrates this idea.

No matter what attitude we adopt, the flow of life continues (from left to right on the diagram). However, right now, in this moment we do have a choice about the direction in which we lean, or move inwardly. Within ourselves, each moment, we can exercise that choice. Each moment is therefore a turning point in which we can reinforce our attitude to be in our favour. We can either lean with the direction that life is moving with a positive attitude, or lean against the direction that life is moving with a negative attitude. When we can go 'with the flow', life becomes easier. When we resist the flow, life becomes more difficult.

In *Set Personal Objectives*, we were exploring a mission; what we want more of in life; a positive focus, with sets of objectives, goals and targets. As you looked to improve the quality of your life, you expanded the vision of what you really want for yourself, a vision that reflects more honestly your values and aspirations.

The exciting truth about human beings is that with the power of imagination and conscious willpower, we can make new choices about creating the future we want for ourselves. Physically, our bodies are designed to move forwards. Our limbs are structured in such a way that we stride ahead more easily than we step backwards. Our eyes are placed in front, so that we look ahead of us, not behind.

Some of our experiences in the past may have caused us to

limit ourselves. However, we need not necessarily be restricted in this way in the future. Sometimes, people age prematurely because they dwell on their past achievements and experiences rather than embrace and enjoy what life currently has to offer them.

As you create an expanded vision for your life, you may find that old attitudes and old beliefs from the past come to the surface in various forms of discouragement. These are the *blocks*, *blocked energy* or *blocked resources* (the left or 'negative' side of the model).

The truth about the past is that there is nothing, with the best will in the world, that you can do to change what has happened. If you think back to something you said an hour ago, or did last week, there is absolutely nothing you can do to make it any different. The past is very much complete in the sense that there is nothing you can do to turn back the clock now. What happened yesterday is already history. You will waste energy by trying to repair the past by analysing and re-living the apparent shortcomings of yourself and others, or by allowing previous unhappy experiences to be carried forward into your vision of tomorrow.

For example, does one bad marriage experience mean that another you enter will similarly 'fail'? Not necessarily, unless perhaps you did not take time to learn with compassion from any errors of your approach to marriage the first time around. Did you drop out of school, or college or university, and doubt your intelligence as a human being? Does your experience of violence as a teenager growing up mean that you have to adopt a violent approach to others as an adult?

It is highly possible that the objectives we set for ourselves may well challenge some of our most entrenched beliefs and approaches. It is in moving courageously forward in our lives that we have the opportunity to heal our former hurts and disappointments.

You may be aware of some exciting developments in the theories of parenthood. When children are behaving in ways that are not socially desirable, instead of being reprimanded, they are re-directed and educated into more positive behaviour. Many children have grown up with a lot of negative commands directed at them as they explored, for the most part innocently, their world. This exploration could have included running out into a busy road, or carving furniture with penknives, or drawing with indelible ink on walls and upholstery, or hitting at the next child to see what reaction that would produce.

As children, in the process of growing up, exploring and learning, we made mistakes for which we were sometimes punished in anger. We may have interpreted the mistake in such a way that we assumed we must be a bad person, or wrong. We took the error in a deeply personal way to be a measure of our lack of goodness, or self-worth.

There are ways in which children can be positively directed out of the area of mistakes, without making heavy weather and blaming them unduly for the results of their curiosity. There are also occasions when discipline needs strong reinforcement. However, even the most enlightened parent is still undergoing his/her own process of discovery in bringing up each child. Children are not born with a set of instructions as to how to raise them.

The point here is that at sometime in your early years, you may have interpreted events as being your 'fault', or against you in some way, or that for some reason you were not quite good enough. These interpretations were possibly seeds for your present set of blocks. For the most part, they may well remain hidden in the unconscious, intangible, while, in ways unseen, they act as a self-regulating mechanism. Rather than be courageous in taking risks, you may hesitate, falter or simply dismiss an area of learning and growth for fear of some negative repercussion that you cannot put your finger on. In some way, the world does not seem safe enough for you.

The key point in the Choice/Attitude Model is that no matter what blocks we have inherited from the past, we can nevertheless choose to go forward, leaning into the direction life is moving with a positive attitude. If we lack the clear vision and goals to look forward to, this may result in our being pulled back into the past with a negative attitude. The simplest way of nurturing a positive attitude within ourselves is to have plenty to look forward to, and to keep reinforcing and refreshing that clear choice. Techniques for strengthening your positive focus are included in subsequent chapters.

An ideal might be to be free of our past experiences, having derived the riches of learning and healing from them; to have a clear view ahead which draws from us our best resources, while enjoying fully whatever we have immediately to hand.

The greatest power we have available to us is that of making clear choices. No matter what is happening in the world around us, we can always potentially *choose* the experience we have within ourselves, within our own inner environment. Even if it is cold and wet outside, if the government have made another dreadful decision, if your partner moaned all weekend about the kids, or your bank manager sent a stiff reminder in the mail, you can still choose how you feel inside. Have you ever felt happy and enthusiastic on a grey wet day? Have you ever cracked up laughing when one thing after another seems to go wrong?

This may be hard to imagine and accept, if you have come to view yourself in some way a victim of your circumstances, seeing the world acting fundamentally against you. This bad condition 'x' is happening in my world, and therefore, I must feel bad in order to be a 'good' person, in empathy with the external, negative conditions. There are usually plenty of people in accord with the negative flow in this way, blaming the boss, government, parents or children for their lack of success and unhappiness. It is a part of the human condition to want to feel at one with our neighbours. However, to club together in negativity is not the most revitalizing option available.

The power of choice does bring with it the freedom of personal accountability, and the direct responsibility for your *experience* of life. Potentially, you have the ability to respond to any circumstance in such a way that your experience of life is an expansive one. You really can choose the mood, the most nurturing inner environment, that will best sustain you in your endeavours.

As you set a new direction for yourself, you may become aware that former activities, even partnerships, are no longer in alignment with your purpose.

Choices

Flexibility and Responsibility

It is always possible
to make new choices

While being accountable for our actions,
we do not have to
endure the consequences
of any choices

We can simply move on to the next choice

and it's fun and free

One of my most remarkable and vivid memories of the power of the human spirit was in India. I was staying in a modest (what a polite expression for it!) hotel in Bombay not far from a building site where the foundations were being laid for a high-rise luxury hotel. From my window, I looked down on a pavement, which at night was covered with people sleeping. During the day, a stretch of no more than two metres was 'inhabited' by a family of four. The mother and father took it in turns to look after their children. Mother worked shifts on the building site by day, carrying loads of earth in a pan on her head. In the evening, she cooked simple meals of lentils, vegetables or whatever they had. They stored their basic utensils behind a wall after they had eaten. Those circumstances were far from elegant, but I noticed on the faces of that family, and of the mother in particular, an extraordinary quality of contentment and pleasure. Now, there is an argument for simple living, but that is not my point here.

How could someone with so little material resource radiate such happiness, when middle-class housewives in the affluent

West, with all the ease and convenience of supermarket shopping (for one thing), moan and complain so much? If successful living were purely a matter of material affluence, then surely those of us who have the basic needs of life taken care of would feel happy and contented.

You can probably recall many examples of the capacity of human beings to overcome the most dreadful of conditions, stories of people with physical ill-health, who nevertheless inspire the rest of us with their courage, innovation and resource. They are only demonstrating the potential we all have in common to triumph over whatever negative conditions we may have to confront.

As we focus forward into an expanded vision for ourselves, blocks will show up as the restraining factors. The categories of blocks are:

1. Comfort Zone

A Comfort Zone encompasses the set of circumstances, the pattern and routine of our life, within which we feel most comfortable and at ease. We become comfortable, for example, with a certain salary or income. We become comfortable with a certain living environment, location and set of friends or work colleagues. When our Comfort Zones are threatened, either by a potential loss (such as loss of job or reduction in salary or separation from a loved one), or even a potential gain (such as an improved lifestyle), a self-regulating mechanism within us strives to return us to the familiar and known Comfort Zone.

The habits and conditions of a Comfort Zone which enable us to function 'on automatic' (such as getting up at a certain time each morning, riding a bicycle, typing, spelling) are very valuable to us.

A Comfort Zone becomes a 'block' when it stands in the way of a new set of choices – thinking, behaviour and results. For example, if you are comfortable with a regular salary, it is 'uncomfortable' for a while to move into your own business, the uncertainty and greater personal responsibility for your income.

2. Deadwood

Deadwood is the mental, emotional and physical clutter that holds our attention in the past because there is some outstanding 'agreed' action not yet taken to resolve it. Similarly, it claims our energy in a backward drift, away from what we are wanting to have more of. It can be easy to understand and deal with. However, if you tend to procrastinate, deadwood can lock you in the past. Handling deadwood effectively is one of the most liberating sources of energy, vitality and creativity that you will ever experience. More about this in *Clear Away Blocks*.

3. Self-Image

As a block, Self-Image is similar to Comfort Zone as it relates to our expectations of life, particularly our expectations relating to how we value ourselves and our capacity to receive.

In one study, a class of first-year university students were asked to write on one side of a sheet of paper all the things they liked about themselves, and on the other side, all the things they did not like about themselves. It was found that on average, the students had six items about themselves that they did not like, for every one that they did.

Self-Image was shown to be a factor that did not necessarily relate to what was considered to be 'intelligence'. A poor self-image reflects a low self-esteem, not low intelligence, and limits the energy we have potentially available to accomplish our success in life, especially our inner success, peace of mind and fulfilment.

In order to begin releasing yourself from some of those blocks, it will be useful to explore what some of them might be. You may be very accomplished in your life, having achieved considerable success in many areas, and yet something inside is not quite satisfied. In spite of your outer success, something inside does not believe it. It may have been that your path to success was costly in terms of stress and anxiety. It could be that no matter how successful you have been, buried deep down are those doubts from years ago, when a parent or teacher criticized you harshly. In your motivation towards your former successes, you might have been carrying the deadweight of some concealed self-doubt as an added burden.

Surfacing Your Limiting Beliefs

This exercise takes willingness and courage, because it is sometimes painful to get in touch with the roadblocks that have seemingly stood in our way in the past. The following examples show the kinds of limiting beliefs that people allow to hold them back in a limited view of themselves. Read them through and allow your own limiting beliefs to surface.

- I was never any good at maths, so I am hopeless at managing my money.
- As a woman, I have to be tough and aggressive to be successful in a man's world.
- My parents never had any money, so I could never be rich.
- I am the sort of person who can never have a really fulfilling marriage – so I'll just make do with what I have.
- I know I will never do anything very spectacular in my career, so I'll do just enough to get by.
- Life is a struggle.
- I never could spell.
- At my age, it is very hard to get a job.

Do you get the idea? In the light of what you want more of, in particular, or in your life generally:

What Are Your Limiting Beliefs?

Take some time, and make a note of the limiting beliefs as they surface. The idea here is absolutely *not* to dwell on them, ingraining them even further, but to be aware of what is holding you back and begin to make some fresh choices for yourself.

With each limiting belief, you have at least two possible approaches that will loosen its hold on you. First of all, a belief that grew up with you may now (based on your life to date) simply no longer be true for you. Delete that statement however you choose and on a fresh sheet of paper, write a positive statement that replaces that old belief.

In the process of doing this, you might like to acknowledge yourself for having overcome the former limiting attitude.

Secondly, you may have limiting beliefs that concern you in the present day and relate to factors about which you have apparently no choice – such as your age, sex, educational background, nationality, skin colour, physical build. The words of your limiting statement can be a valuable guide in defining a preferred choice, an expanding statement, for yourself. This exercise can best be applied to your most deeply-felt goals or objectives. Just trying to prove a point, one way or another, is not a very substantial motivation. Begin to adjust your attitude to view any apparently limiting circumstance as being positively an asset in your favour.

In making expanding statements, remember that any worthwhile vision, goal or objective must be 'within your reach, but not within your grasp' so that there is some movement, or motivation, involved in getting what you are going after. Be sensitive and selective in your choice of words.

Keep somewhere for your easy reference these positive, expanding statements. This is a way of recording your preferences and having a reminder of the direction in which you are heading. Burn, shred, destroy, however you wish, the limiting ones.

The following examples illustrate a former limiting belief which you have now overcome:

1. Limiting belief:
I will always be overweight.
Accurate, present day statement:
I am now fitter than I have ever been through taking regular exercise and enjoying a diet that maintains an acceptable bodyweight.
Acknowledgement:
I appreciate that I practised consistent discipline in getting to my preferred body weight and I now really enjoy better health.
2. Limiting belief:
If I am 'lucky in money', I will never be 'lucky in love'.
Accurate, present day statement:
My business is going sufficiently well that I spend fewer hours working at it, and have time to enjoy with my family and friends.
Acknowledgement:
It was worth putting in those extra hours of effort at the beginning of my career to have a heightened enjoyment of my life now.

These next examples illustrate a change of attitude when you think that you have apparently no choice to effect changes.

1. Limiting belief:
I am too old to get a job.
Expanding statement:
There are interesting and rewarding jobs for me, where the experience of my age, my reliability and commitment is a great advantage.
2. Limiting belief:
I dropped out of school at 14 and do not have

> sufficient education to enjoy a worthwhile career.
>
> **Expanding statement:**
> I can study now for the qualifications I need to pursue my love of working with animals.

The last exercise introduces two important concepts.

1. Expansion vs. contraction
2. The influence of words upon our reality

When you are leaning into the flow of your life, making positive choices, there is a quality of expansion and openness, excitement and enthusiasm. The expanding statements open you to new possibilities. Like a helium balloon, you can lift above the blocks and gain greater perspective and vision. The limiting beliefs, or statements of contraction, literally condense the energy you have available to you, so your tendency is to sink like a stone.

When you choose to focus positively on your objectives, the qualities you want more of in life, your energies expand and you literally feel lighter. On the other hand, negative feelings and emotions produce tension, stress and heaviness. The flow of energy circulating in our bodies gets blocked and the physical result is 'dis-ease'. Mentally and emotionally, the blocked energy is experienced as some form of 'depression', to put it simply. A lack of appetite for any aspect of life, boredom or apathy, for example, would reflect to you a state of contraction.

An analogy is that of either being in a valley with high mountains all around you limiting your vision, or alternatively, climbing up the mountain so that you can see for miles around and can clearly choose from all the options available within sight. The higher you lift above your circumstances, the greater your view, and the more numerous your choices. You might imagine yourself in a hot air balloon, rising above the ground. The higher you lift, the more you can see. So if you find yourself feeling trapped with limited options, look for a way of lifting above the situation.

The following is an exercise to demonstrate a simple way of expanding into your well-being.

Look Up, Or Look Down, It's Your Choice!

Sit in a chair, with your arms and legs crossed, and hunched up as much as possible, looking down with your chin on your chest. Say the following words aloud:

Joy, happiness, enthusiasm, fun.

How does that feel?

Now stand up and stretch, look up and say these words:

Misery, depression, sadness.

Those words may not feel so bad for you. Notice how the way you hold your body influences how you feel. Making simple adjustments to your posture may influence your successful outcomes in life. Your body language 'talks' as much to you as to other people.

As a final part to this exercise, stand up, stretch and (provided circumstances allow) look up, and say, as loudly as you dare, imagining yourself projecting your voice across a huge stadium:

Terrific, great, brilliant, love.

If you are not feeling as enthusiastic and as happy as you would like, try changing your posture and improving your circulation.

Notice how sitting around in a state of inactivity will produce within you a greater experience of contraction or discouragement, even depression. Simply getting up and getting going can, in that instant, transform the quality of your life.

Another way of nurturing greater feelings of expansion and well-being within yourself is through your use of language. The words you use have a significant impact on you. The thoughts you turn over in your mind can contract, or expand, the energy you have available to you. If you think happy thoughts, you will begin to feel happier. If you dwell on negative thoughts, you will become discouraged. For example, start thinking of all the things you cannot do and notice how your mood begins to sink.

So the next time you are feeling less than optimistic, say the words: *happy* or *joy* or *fun* or *bliss*, over and over again in your mind, or better still out aloud if you are on your own or you don't mind a reaction from others around you. At least, consciously bring a smile to your face, and notice how you feel differently. Smiling alone may make you more relaxed. Remember the last occasion you really laughed.

Nurturing a more positive attitude, or frame of mind, is now a choice you can be consciously making as you expand towards your objectives. As you become more aware of the signs of limitation or contraction in the words you use, you can switch your thinking so that it reflects and opens into a positive focus. Choose the words and expressions that most support your expansion.

You may be familiar with the idea of self-fulfilling prophecy, or as you think, so you become. 'Whether you think you can, or you think you can't, you are probably right' as the saying goes. With the attitude of 'I can . . .' and 'I will . . .', you open yourself to possibilities.

As you start turning towards a new, more positive direction, old self-doubts may begin to surface, temporarily producing a sense of chaos and feelings of confusion. This may not feel very comfortable for you. However, in order to create anything new, such a period of confusion is very natural as you detach yourself from the habitual patterns of thinking and behaviour which would conflict with your new vision.

There is an emotional pattern sometimes experienced in progressing towards new goals and a new lifestyle. The pattern can be similar to that experienced at any major turning point in life.

The change of circumstances could be one that you have consciously chosen, such as
getting married
starting a new job
relocating.

Or, alternatively, the changes could be those 'imposed' on you, such as:
getting divorced
being fired from your job
death of a loved one.

With each circumstance, there is a process of adjustment, even if that is not apparent at the outset, and that process can be stressful. What we are looking at primarily is the **positive** area of your new vision and objectives.

There is a process of change that happens within you. Being aware of what happens during a period of change, recognizing it, and handling the process constructively is the key to going through it successfully.

To illustrate this, you might first imagine that your current circumstances are represented by a country in which you are now living. In this case, you are choosing a new improved lifestyle, which is represented by another land overseas.

You might experience some anticipation and a thrill as you prepare to begin. You may even feel quite high, perhaps even a little detached from reality, as if you were floating on 'cloud nine', as the new vision forms in your mind. The initial excitement and enthusiasm of a new scheme may lead to a honeymoon period and some over-expectation. You envisage, for example, the new business operating successfully, and your achievement with it. The future has a rosy glow to it. Your energy is high and you are ready to embark upon your new venture. This might also apply to the first day of a new diet, starting a new school with a new school uniform, or even the early days of retirement.

A bank manager, retiring after 40 years of a respectable career in the community, feels (and sometimes behaves) like a schoolboy on the first day of the summer holidays. He may live in a cloud of euphoria and optimism for months, somewhat out of touch with the real world around him.

Then you could imagine making the sea crossing towards your new land of opportunity, the destination of your more fulfilling lifestyle. This stage of adjustment is a period of the unknown.

Some days, it is plain sailing. The sun is in the sky and although you know you have not yet arrived, the journey feels pleasant. There may be other days when the seas are stormy and unpredictable. Emotionally, you may feel caught in a gale over which you have no control. The nights could seem long and dark and you may even feel the extreme of panic attacks of 'maybe this ship won't make it'.

The unknown typically produces within us an experience of fear. We feel most comfortable when we know what is going on, and preferably, have some control over it.

Another difficult emotion we may encounter is that of doubt: doubt about our capacity for effecting our vision, even doubt about ourselves as worthwhile people. Then we may also experience from time to time, a range of mixed feelings which seem to be quite irrational, such as anger, guilt, resentment, disappointment. We may even experience forms of grief, even if what we are leaving behind is something we no longer want. Misunderstandings and hurt feelings may surface unexpectedly in our relations with friends and loved ones.

Sometimes, changing circumstances are not felt consciously, but may unconsciously upset your normal appetites, sleeping habits and body weight.

You might find something in the nature of an 'inner rebellion' going on as on the one hand you want to create a new set of circumstances for yourself, and on the other, you are reluctant to let go of the old. You may hear yourself saying something like the following:

- If only things were the same as before . . .
- If only I had done 'x', then 'y' wouldn't be happening
- I wish I had never started on this project – life was nice and simple before
- I don't think I am doing the right thing
- I wish I could turn the clock back
- I feel confused
- I don't know what's going on
- If only I had been a more loving wife/husband/father/ mother/daughter/son . . .
- Perhaps this is all a mistake

Even though intellectually, we are in accord with our aims, emotionally there may be a feeling of upset. A very down-to-earth career woman who retired in her late 50s reported having irrational feelings of anger and irritation. She would be standing in a queue in the post office, and for no logical reason, suddenly feel intense fury towards the person standing in front of her. Another example is when all the excitement and anticipation of a new baby is followed by the severe mixed feelings of post-natal depression.

It can be at these times, when we think we *should* be acting rationally, and become over-critical of ourselves, that we resist the flow of what is happening. As you move towards a more successful lifestyle, you may feel uncertain at times. What you will need to assist you is a source of both inner and outer support and encouragement.

When you are sailing on an emotional ocean, all the positive thinking in the world does not always have much effect. However, no matter what the daily conditions bring, you can keep your vessel on course for your destination with *positive focusing*. Affirmations and Power Statements, described in later chapters, assist you in vividly reinforcing and keeping in sight your destination, giving you encouragement to weather any storms.

As you keep your eyes focused on your chosen objectives, you will minimize any emotional discomfort. As you learn to observe any mixed feelings that surface, you may be able to discover that what first appeared to be a distraction was really a blessing in disguise.

A way of releasing blocked energy, or utilizing these periods of resistance, is to imagine the 'block' as a form, visually. For example, suppose you were feeling literally 'knotted up', like a ball of tangled wool. You could imagine yourself holding the ball of wool and gently easing out the single strands from the tangle. As the strands of wool clearly separate, you might recognize the qualities that those strands represent to you. Then, rather than focus on the resistance, you might choose to reinforce the qualities contained within what first appeared as a block.

As you grow into the new, larger picture of your life, you may push against old barriers and old walls rather like a butterfly emerging from a protective cocoon. You might also view a block as being like an oyster shell, rough and hard to open. However, contained in the oyster shell is the beauty of the pearl. Similarly, the apparently lifeless form of an egg contains the new life of a bird that can fly high.

If you do feel your attitude becoming locked in with feelings of resistance, doubt, fear, discouragement or simply confusion, it is possible to take a new look and gain fresh inspiration.

The next exercise is one of creative visualization, that will use the capacity you have for drawing upon, and expanding, your wealth of inner resources. For the best results, give yourself at least 10 minutes alone, with absolutely no distractions. Take the phone off the hook, close the door and make sure that on no account are you disturbed. As before, you may wish to put the words of the visualization onto a cassette so that you can sit comfortably in an easy chair, with your eyes closed, and allow your imagination to flow freely. Allow sufficient time between each phrase to bring the images to mind.

Transforming Your Attitude Towards Your Blocks

Sitting comfortably, take in a very deep breath, hold it for a moment and let it out with a sigh . . . Once again, take in a deep breath, and as you do so, breathe in a relaxation . . . let that breath out with a sigh, letting go of any distractions, thoughts, concerns . . . begin to feel a peacefulness entering you . . . this time is for you alone . . . Notice if there are places of tightness or tension in your body . . . any aches . . . breathe into them . . . and let them go . . . you do not have to do anything with them . . . just observe them if they are there . . . How are you feeling? Observe your feelings . . . and let them go . . . Notice how your feelings change . . . and move on . . . Observe your breath . . . notice how it comes and goes . . . you do not have to do anything with it . . . it just happens . . . notice the rhythm of your breathing . . . the ease of your life force . . .

Bring to mind now a situation in which you have felt blocked . . . or confusion . . . Allow that block to take some specific form in your imagination . . . What is that form? . . . Is it a wall . . . a huge rock . . ? Something else . . ? What do you notice about the form? . . . Is it warm or cold? . . . Hard or soft to touch? . . . Does it have any colour, or colours? . . . Light or dark? . . . Are there any sounds with this form? . . .

If you can, and would like to, take the form in your hands . . . Allow warmth from your hands to go into the form . . . You might also like to envisage a clear white light to surround the form . . . Begin now to see it clearly for what it truly is . . . Using your hands to assist the process of transformation . . . or simply allowing it to open of its own . . . notice an opening up . . . emerging . . . releasing . . . into a new form . . . there may be colours, shapes, qualities that you notice as the new form unfolds in your hands . . . Notice the finest details as they appear to you . . .

> *Looking at this new form now . . . What are the qualities that are now available to you? . . . What are the strengths that you now see . . . that were previously hidden? . . . There may be two or three words that come to mind now . . . Get in touch with these qualities . . . breathe into them and watch them expand . . . breathe into these qualities until they fill you . . . let these qualities into every cell of your body . . . so that you radiate them within you . . . and outside of you . . .*
>
> *See yourself walking . . . with these qualities guiding you . . . Hear yourself talking . . . with these qualities enthusing your language . . . Feel yourself . . . fully enjoying the best that these qualities have to enrich your life . . .*
>
> *Now, with these new qualities still very much living within you . . . very gently, gradually and in your own timing . . . become aware of the room you are in . . . and open your eyes . . .*
>
> *Take a notebook, and make any notes that you would like about the qualities you have received, and how you will draw on these resources to enhance your process of change . . .*

Your former 'limitations' or blocks are truly rich resources. In time, your resources will increase as they become known and useful to you, especially as you progress towards your new pictures of success. The more you come to use your resources, the more you will value them, and yourself, in the process. Whatever it was that previously restrained you can evolve into a wealth of vitality, information, gifts and talents. The main choice you always have is in the attitude you adopt towards whatever is happening in the present moment.

You might like to consider the following:

The real block is not what *is happening, but* how we relate *to what is happening.*

How you relate to yourself, while you are experiencing a block, is the block.

Blocks are perhaps in one sense a form of handicap. You are

probably aware of people, 'incapacitated' in some way, who develop a sixth sense or extra ability for getting on in life, such as the blind, or deaf and, remarkably these days, children with cerebral palsy. The work being done for paraplegic children by the Peto Institute in Budapest is an inspiration of the capacity of the human spirit, given warmth, encouragement, loving and opportunity. Children, for whom hope of an independent life had formerly been given up, demonstrate the achievement of physical mobility, which could only be looked upon as 'miraculous'.

Attitude and belief are keys to their accomplishment. Perhaps for those who do not have an obvious 'handicap', the greatest frontiers and barriers are those unseen by the physical eye and carried unconsciously within the mental and emotional makeup. Similarly, with warmth, encouragement and loving we can overcome our inner blocks.

Your inner world is where you have the greatest freedom to explore, create and develop. No one has access to your secret thoughts, unless you choose to reveal them. It does not matter if from time to time you feel less than confident. The value of feeling shaky, or unsure, is that you will test carefully the ground ahead of you before you tread on it. Once you know your weak spots, you know where you need to build more inner strength.

There is an experiment which demonstrates vividly the relationship between your inner environment and the response of your body. It uses a process called appplied kinesiology or muscle testing. See for yourself with the following exercise how this works.

Muscle Testing For Expansion

Start by touching together the tips of your right-hand thumb and little finger so they cannot be prised apart. Test the strength of their holding by placing your left-hand thumb and forefinger within the 'loop' formed by your right thumb and little finger, and trying to prise them apart.

Now, run some negative self-talk through your mind along the lines of:

I am a bad person, I will never achieve what I want in life, I am a failure, I am not very worthwhile, I hate myself . . .

Once again, hold your right thumb and little finger together and check whether your left thumb and forefinger can prise them apart. You will probably notice a weakening in those muscles of your right hand.

Shake both your hands out, shake your fingers.

Now, run some warm, loving, encouraging words through your mind:

I am warm, loving and capable, I have all that I need to achieve great success in my life, I am a very good person, I am strong and can easily overcome any obstacle . . . etc.

Repeat the test with your fingers and notice the greater strength in your muscles. This simple choice of language will prepare your attitude for expansion, for the success you seek.

There has been considerable work done in this area which demonstrates how powerfully our words, thoughts and imagery influence our physiological makeup. Negative thinking and attitudes can literally deplete us, physically, mentally and emotionally. If your purpose is now to enjoy living successfully:

You cannot afford the luxury of a negative thought.

A positive thought that you might like to entertain, regularly, on your path to success is:

At all times, I am doing the best I can at the time. If I knew better, I would do better.

Given that on the path to your success, the road may become

bumpy at times, what might be your best approach? You might begin by accepting that here you have a situation that needs constructive attention, not contracting away from. Then you might ask yourself, how can I adopt a positive attitude towards it, instead of pulling away from it? What is the gain, or the benefit it is bringing to me? How would I handle this situation if I had all the money in the world? What would my attitude be then? What is there here for me to learn? How can I be grateful for this issue?

As you take charge over your inner environment, accepting and addressing your doubts, fears and concerns, you will have a greater impact in the outer world of the results you produce. **Any challenge that you face can be transformed into an advantage, any problem is potentially a gift.**

For example, if you wanted to progress an innovative business venture which was as yet untried and unproven in your marketplace as a whole, you are likely to be met with a variety of 'obstacles' in the forms of resistance from your potential buyers. They have no evidence that what you say is so. Your word is against their doubt. This could turn out to be deeply discouraging and frustrating.

Emotionally, you might even pick up some feelings of doubt yourself, even though you know and are convinced of the validity of your product or service. Failures to sell it could be taken inwardly as personal rejection, with a reaction from you that wants to reject those others, and make 'them' wrong, bad or just plain stupid. The personal rejection could, alternatively, be turned with an open mind into an opportunity for discovering new ways of selling your enterprise. It is on these occasions that you most need your network of friends, colleagues and supporters to assist you over the hurdles and clarify your best plan of action.

The next exercise is about transforming a doubting attitude or belief into a step towards a new set of results in your life. The purpose is to anticipate an inner block towards an objective you have set. This limiting belief may be currently hidden to you, and by becoming aware of it, you can turn it into a new positive experience, by agreeing an action that you will take.

Choosing Your Choice

This exercise can be done using a pen and paper to make notes as you go from 1 to 7. The exercise is not complete, however, until you start taking action in the world, based on your answers.

1. Bring a goal or objective to mind.
2. What limiting belief or statement blocks you from achieving your goal?
3. What preferred view would you like to choose for yourself in the place of the limitation?
4. Make a simple positive statement of your new chosen attitude.
5. What is the first, simple action you will take to demonstrate, primarily to yourself, your new choice?
6. When will you take that action?
7. How will you reward yourself for completing that first action?

It will take more than one action to replace the thinking and habits of a lifetime. As you complete one action, then look for the next and do that one too. And so on until you are confidently in place with a new set of experiences and beliefs about yourself.

This step-by-step process will assist you in getting to grips with what you want for yourself, surfacing any fears or doubts that might be lurking unconsciously within you and, most importantly, committing you to the vital first step that will take you forward in the direction of your choice.

The following examples illustrate this exercise:

1. Goal
   I would like to have my own house, with a garden.

2. Limiting Belief
As a woman in administration, I am not worth the kind of salary that would enable me to cover the payments on a one bedroom apartment, far less a house with a garden.

3. Preferred View
I am very good at my job and I have some very good ideas that could improve the profitability of the company.

4. Positive Statement
I am worth the kind of salary that would enable me to buy the kind of house I would enjoy living in.

5. First Action
I will re-evaluate my job, and my worth to the company, in the light of the additional contribution I can be making now.

6. When
I will take a hour next Saturday to sit down and work this out, and take more time if necessary.

7. My Reward
I will reward myself by going to the movies with some friends in the evening.

1. Goal
I want to learn to become a pilot.

2. Limiting Belief
At 55 I am too old to learn; after all, you can't teach an old dog new tricks.

3. Preferred View
I can gain so much pleasure and enjoyment from applying my patience and discipline in becoming an excellent solo pilot.

4. Positive Statement
I love the exhilaration of flying a Cessna single-handed.

> **5. First Action**
> I will find out all the requirements I need to begin lessons in flying, and how much that will cost.
> **6. When**
> By the end of this month.
> **7. My Reward**
> I will buy aircraft magazines and go window shopping for a smart little plane.

The previous exercise leads to the following equation:

Choice + Action = Experience = Understanding/Belief

A first step is choosing the most positive frame of mind, or inner environment. The next step is deciding how you can best support your internal well-being. Then, most importantly, is taking the appropriate external action that brings life and form to your positive intention.

With an open mind and your goals and objectives in view, every action you take, and every experience that results, is potentially a gain that will bring you closer to where you want to be.

The understanding that you gain from your own experiences is a great source of strength for you. Your experiences may not be universally the same as those of other people, but no one can deny you the validity of your own experience. Only you will know what your experiences have been for you and how they have personally enriched you. It is the interpretation of your experiences that will colour your understanding and appreciation of them, favourably or otherwise.

For example, consider Edison, inventing the electric light bulb. The story goes that he had 1,000 or more attempts before he arrived at his 'solution'. Each negative result in his experimentation would have given him understanding, if only of what did not work. Had he given up in discouragement and stopped taking action, he would not have succeeded.

In *Create Inner Strength*, you will discover other ways of enhancing your inner environment. For now, here are some simple suggestions:

Maintaining a Positive Attitude

1. Humour

The most successful people are those who keep a sparkle in their eye; those who, while taking their goals and aims in life seriously, nevertheless do not lose sight of the larger perspective in life, their fallibility and humanness.

Make space for more laughter! Be selective in the television you watch. Why not switch off the news, often negative in quality, and choose more comedy? Humour is explored more fully in *Simply Have Fun*. For now, observe how laughter contributes to your increased well-being.

2. Gratitude

One way of building your sense of gratitude is to: 'Count your blessings.' It is especially useful to remember to do this during a period of change, when you seem to be more aware of what you are losing, and the gains have yet to show up.

At these times, take a break from what you have been doing and go for a walk, counting as you go all the small things you usually take for granted. The exercise is very simple. It goes something like this:

I am grateful for my health,
I am grateful for having enough food to eat today,
I am grateful for my family,
I am grateful for my husband,
I am grateful for my friends,
I am grateful for the education I received,

I am grateful for the roof over my head,
I am grateful for . . .

What is important here is not the magnitude of each item, but the number of items that you can count. Each item counted seems to expand the degree of fullness or feeling of abundance. Your inner wealth will expand. With that expansion inwardly comes the greater vision and freedom to move into the direction of your choice.

3. Exercise/Action

During periods of change, a certain lethargy can sometimes accompany a lack of clarity and confusion about life. Too much sitting about makes for more tiredness, low energy, lack of inspiration and procrastination. A very helpful discipline is to spend, say, 15 minutes a day doing some kind of non-strenuous, enjoyable exercise, such as walking or swimming.

Physical movement is expansive. Simply a change of scene can change your perspective and lend a whole new set of possibilities to your circumstances. Taking action to deal with the most basic needs in your life also releases new energy to you. More about taking action in *Clear Away Blocks*.

4. Future Focus

If maintaining a positive attitude has to do with maintaining our flow in the direction of life, towards what we want more of, then a very simple thing to do is to plan, in the short term, and the long term if possible, something to look forward to.

Your objectives and specific goals may not yet be in shape. Nevertheless, find things to do that will give you pleasure. Plan a meal with friends; or to go to a movie, concert or art gallery; a trip to the country, park or seaside; a massage, game of golf, or beauty treatment.

5. Language

The final tip concerns the language you use. Choose your words wisely. Have fun with them. One of the delightful aspects of the 'English' language is that it has been adapted within the many cultures that speak it. As cultures grow and evolve, the language, a living entity, changes to match the new form. Above all, speak kind words to yourself as you nurture the expansion within you, as you grow towards your goals.

In later chapters, there are techniques called *Affirmations* and *Power Statements*, concerning the use of language. These are statements designed by you to assist you in attracting to you more of what you want. For now, the following exercise is one to experiment with. Notice the expansion that takes place within you as you do it.

Expansion Statements

Complete the following statements in a notebook:

- I am proud that I . . .
- My greatest strength is . . .
- Something I do well is . . .
- I have the power to . . .
- If I want to, I can . . .
- I have accomplished . . .
- Something I am getting better at is . . .
- My greatest asset is . . .
- I am happiest when I . . .

One of the greatest benefits of having an older generation is that we can learn from their experience of life, and avoid making some of the mistakes they may have made in gaining their wisdom.

A delightful example in the area of attitude was a lady with whom I travelled as part of a group of some 120 people through Israel and Egypt. That journey had its moments of irritation and frustration, when other travellers' personal behaviour, or the standards of accommodation, did not match my particular expectations or needs. I found myself more than once feeling moody and resentful.

At such times, I noticed this particular woman, older than most of the group, and with a physical 'disability' in her legs, radiant and smiling, taking every condition, negative or positive, in her stride. I could rely upon her to be noticing something good or beautiful in every location, no matter what was going on. She was always grateful. She could always find something to be grateful for. That was her outlook.

She demonstrated very vividly that:

> *The attitude of gratitude*
> *is an essential key*
> *to successful living*

Unlocking your attitude begins with realizing that you have the power to choose, at all times, to focus positively on what you are wanting more of, on your vision, objectives and goals. Your attitude, in each moment, has a direct influence on the quality of your life. As you build, strengthen and develop within you a battery of *constructive emotion,* and direct that energy in appropriate *action* towards your aims, then you are well on your way to experiencing successful living.

Chapter 3

Clear Away Blocks

As has been mentioned earlier, at all points in creating a more successful life for yourself, you may find yourself confronting blocks. Right at the beginning, in getting to know what it is you really want, you may have found yourself coming up with lots of good reasons why you cannot have it. In fact, some of us so doubt that we can have what we most want, that we do not dare to contemplate what we consider to be the 'impossible'.

Our blocks can serve a very valuable purpose. When you encounter a good reason that blocks you from moving ahead, there are two ways of viewing it. One is that in your heart of hearts, you do not really want to move ahead in that particular direction. The second is that it is a real block that needs to be overcome, but that it is also a real source of information. You may be stopped in your tracks because there is something you need to think through more clearly.

In this chapter, blocks are going to be reviewed in a positive light in the following areas.

1. Often the immediate responses, either inwardly or outwardly, towards making a change for the better will concern the blocks of:

time

money or

other people.

These are factors, apparently outside ourselves, over which we have no control, and therefore render us incapable of movement.

2. In the Choice/Attitude Model in *Unlock Your Attitude,* the blocked energy or resources from the past which hold us back from progressing towards our goals and objectives are:

Deadwood
Self-Image
Comfort Zone

3. Blocks in our communications and relationships with others can be turned into resources.

4. When we choose to expand towards having more of what we want in our lives, we are often confronted with feelings of lack, blocks which can colour and limit our outlook.

Many of the most powerful blocks are truly within us. When we are clearly in line with what we truly want, the world almost falls at its feet to give it to us. The chapter concludes with some inner remedies for the inner blocks. As we open the space within ourselves to receive more fully, all the resources we need become more available to us.

As you contemplate a more desirable future for yourself, you may come up with one or more of the blocks as 'reasons' why you cannot have what you most want:

1. Time

- I do not have enough time to . . .
- There are not enough hours in the day . . .
- It will take too long.

2. Money

- I cannot afford . . .
- I have to have xyz in the bank before I do this . . .
- There are other priorities for my money
- We could not live on less than xyz income per month

• My parents would cut off my allowance if I . . .

3. Other People

• My husband/wife could not manage if I . . .
• My children need me at home . . .
• My boss wouldn't let me . . .
• No one would employ me afterwards if it went wrong . . .
• I would lose my friends if . . .
• I might lose my credibility if . . .
• People would cease to respect me . . .

If these kinds of considerations are coming to mind, it could be that they are valid for you and it is important that you honour them. The objectives you have been contemplating are probably not sufficiently important for you at this point in your life. If, however, the doubts are more like excuses for not progressing, while underneath you really do want to effect changes in your life, then you will need to address and resolve them.

Let us explore each of these three issues in turn:

1. Time

This is a matter of learning to manage your time better or, to put it more accurately, learning to manage yourself better in the time you have available.

Here are some questions for you to consider and begin to clarify for yourself:

• Are you spending time on what you consider to be a priority?
• Are you spending time on tasks which could be as well, or even better, accomplished by others?
• Do you have difficulty saying 'no' when people want to spend time with you?
• How can you make the time you spend with others more enjoyable and productive?

- Could you manage with less sleep at night?
- How could you simplify your life and reduce the commitments on your time?
- Do you have too many 'irons in the fire' or more commitments than you can reasonably manage?

2. Money

Concerns about money, especially the lack of it, are very real for most of us. Yet when we are actively engaged in something that absorbs us and gives us pleasure money is less of a concern, provided our basic needs are taken care of.

Managing your money, like managing your time, is more a matter of managing yourself better in relation to the money you have available. Looking at it from the simplest point of view, if you need more money in your life, you need either to spend less, or to earn more, or both.

If the question of money raises itself as an issue in setting objectives for yourself, you can use it to clarify your deepest motivations.

Imagine for a moment that you have all the money you could possibly need, or even want. Bring a figure to mind. What would you buy? Houses, cars, boats, holidays, university education for the children? Have a field day and think of everything you could possibly want to purchase. As you do this, you might also bear in mind the responsibility – not just financial – you would have for the upkeep of some of these possessions. You and your dependents are provided for so that you no longer have to work for an income. When you have done that part of the exercise, you still have a lot of money left over. What will you do with it, and most importantly, yourself, now?

An example of someone who did this exercise was a person who, when he had spent all he could possibly imagine, thought that what he would like to do with the surplus money was to sponsor creative people, such as painters, poets and writers, to produce their work. He subsequently discovered that he did not need money to encourage people to perform and create their work. His career became directed into assisting people, not just artists, into fulfilling their creative ambitions.

Another example was a painter who earned a living through teaching, who became very certain that he wanted to devote his time to his creative work, and in the course of sharing his dream, he met a sponsor who supported him for a year to produce his work for sale in a gallery in Florence.

Being very clear about what you most want can assist you considerably with any block about money. When you want something strongly enough, money need not be the issue.

3. Other People

As with time and money, the doubts raised by others, especially those close to us, serve to clarify what we truly want. You may notice that the concerns that other people raise match closely your deep-seated fears and bring them to the surface.

When you are clear about what you want, you will probably find it easier to answer any doubts raised by others. What is more, when you are fired with your own enthusiasm and excitement, you may well find people only too happy to support and encourage you. Enthusiasm is contagious and people usually welcome it. They will enjoy being in the presence of your vitality.

More about other people as your assets later.

One of the greatest blocks we can encounter is 'circulation failure', and it is one over which we can exercise direct control. Many of us are acquisitive by nature. We gather around us projects, possessions, assorted commitments, savings of one sort or another in case one day we have need of them. However, much of the stuff that accumulates around us acts as an invisible trap for our time, personal resources and vitality.

The Action/Productivity Cycle demonstrates the value to keep 'circulating' and moving on in life (Figure 4).

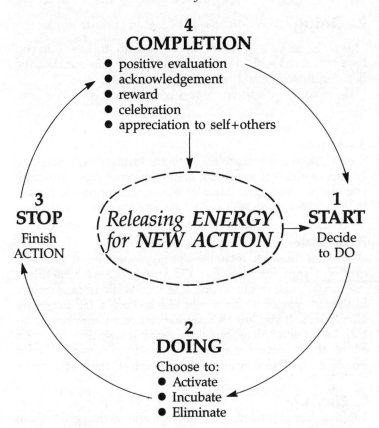

Figure 4: Action/Productivity Cycle

1. Start

Any time you decide you are going to do something, mentally and emotionally you become involved in bringing about that outcome. It is something that happens unconsciously. Even if it is only a thought, some of your unconscious attention will go towards resolving the wish.

2. Doing

This is the active part where, in response to the intention you have registered with your unconscious self, you translate the decision to action and reality in your world.

There are always three choices with any decision you have made:

A. Activate

When you activate a project, you are involved in a series of actions that lead to achieving the results you want. Although you may not be engaged full-time on any one project, you are in charge of the progress and timing of each one, step by step.

B. Incubate

When you choose to incubate a project, you are not yet ready to give it your full attention. Or, you may have some ideas which you need to put to one side for a while until you have further information. You might like to keep a file for Pretty Good Ideas. If you are an imaginative person who comes up with lots of good ideas, but simply do not have the time to do all of them, you would put yourself on 'overload', and experience pressure by attempting to activate them all at once.

C. Eliminate

You may have initiated some projects and having given them careful consideration, decide that you do not wish to pursue them. A 'project' need not be on a grand scale. You may for example decide not to mend a piece of china, but rather throw it away. Then there is the book you have been meaning to read for weeks: you can consciously decide not to read it.

3. Stop

This is where the action is complete. There is no more to be done because the result you set out to achieve has now been accomplished.

4. Completion

This is a valuable stage in the cycle of action because it indicates to your unconscious that the idea, project, venture, task is now concluded. Completion is an act which demonstrates the conclusion so that no more unconscious attention is absorbed. As you demonstrate completion to yourself, more unconscious energy is released and becomes available to you to direct into new endeavours.

Completion brings about an experience within you of expansion and a sense of satisfaction as the energy, committed to a former enterprise, is 'free' again. The act of completion is like that of closing a door on one phase of activity, enabling another door to open.

Looking at a cycle of action on a large scale, such as the period of time covering a working career, or part of one, completion might take the form of a positive stocktake, acknowledgement and appreciation expressed to yourself and others, and possibly a leaving celebration of some kind like a party, or special holiday. On a smaller scale, such as finishing a series of household tasks, completion might take the form of ticking items off a list.

The idea of appreciating and rewarding ourselves for what we have achieved contributes a great deal to our experience of successful living. All too often, we are more aware of our shortcomings and failures. You may be someone who is more accustomed to punishing yourself for what you failed to do, rather than rewarding yourself for your successes. When we punish ourselves, our energy becomes depleted and we experience stress in some form.

Appreciation and reward are explored more fully in later chapters. However, for now, you might like to reflect on the following questions:

How will you reward yourself when you achieve your goals? How will you celebrate the completion of your targets?

Each step, each target, you accomplish on the way to your goals could be viewed as a separate cycle of action. Each action you take may be acknowledged in some way, even when the end result is not precisely as you had envisaged. As you complete each stage, you will refresh your supplies of energy and enthusiasm and maintain your sense of purpose and direction.

The next exercise addresses stages (2) and (4) of the Action/Productivity Cycle. You may well have had the experience of moving house, perhaps more than once, in your life. In which case, you might recall that in the process of moving, you discarded many household effects that you no longer used nor wanted, but were not aware of in your original home. You may have looked into a cupboard under the stairs, an attic, cellar or corner of the garage and thrown away sacks full of rusty equipment, children's toys, notebooks from college days, broken garden furniture.

Moving into a new lifestyle is similar to moving house in this respect. There may be any amount of household equipment, personal clothing and effects and outstanding actions yet to be taken that do not fit into your vision of the future. This clutter, or deadwood, literally holds us back in the past and inhibits our progress into the future of our choice. What is more, if you are finding difficulty in clarifying your objectives, it may be that there is too much 'deadwood' in your unconscious for you to be able to see forward clearly.

These outstanding commitments, unfinished projects, clutter in your home, bills to be paid, communications to be made, books and journals to be read, filing to be done, clothes to be thrown out and repair work to be done are all examples of deadwood in your environment which will stand in the way of your clear thinking. One of the simplest ways of gaining inner clarity is to take action, and clear up something in your physical environment.

Whether or not you have clarified your objectives and a plan of action, the exercise of Clearing Out The Deadwood is the simplest and most effective for lifting above your current circumstances and gaining greater perspective. The first step is to identify the 'deadwood' in your life.

Clearing Out The Deadwood – What Is Your Deadwood?

The first part of this exercise is simply becoming aware of the deadwood around you. This is a process of identifying as many items as possible that are between (1) and (2) on the Action/Productivity Cycle. It is not a commitment to do anything about it at this stage.

Take a page in a notebook, and make notes of any deadwood that comes to mind in response to the following questions:

- Do you have any outstanding projects at home?
    e.g. clearing out the garage, sewing or knitting, insulating the roof, decorating a room, installing heating/air conditioning/water softener etc.
- Do you have any outstanding correspondence?
    e.g. letters to family and friends, legal or financial matters etc.
- Do you have any payments due?
    e.g. insurance renewal, loan repayments, etc.
- Do you have any money owing to you?
    e.g. loans from friends, refunds, payment for goods or services etc.
- Do you have any clothes that you no longer wear?
- Are there any household or personal effects that you no longer use or want?
    e.g. cooking utensils, furniture, ornaments, golf clubs, books, magazines, cardboard boxes, toys, etc.
- Is there anything you have been meaning to do and have not yet done?
    e.g. take the children to the zoo, go to a movie, buy some new shoes, have lunch with a friend.

- Do you have any outstanding communications to be made with family, friends or work colleagues?
- Are there any appointments you need to make?
  e.g. Dentist, doctor, hairdresser, etc.
- Do you have any cupboards, closets, filing cabinets, drawers that need clearing out?
- Are there any areas at work that need repair, maintenance or cleaning?

Preparing such a list is quite a challenge sometimes because we encounterer the resistances that may have blocked us from taking the action in the first place. You might like to look upon this first stage of the exercise as an action in itself, and agree a reward for yourself when you finish it. Make sure you do give yourself the reward, but only when you have finished.

It may seem simplistic, but setting up a reward system for yourself is a great way to overcome the inertia in getting started on some actions which are less appealing to you.

Clearing Out The Deadwood – Activate, Incubate, Eliminate

The next stage of the exercise addresses (2) on the Action/Productivity Cycle. You might like to begin, by crossing out, each item that you are not going to give any more attention. This is not to say that at some time in the future, you may not decide to read that book, have lunch with that person, mend that cupboard, but for now those are no longer in your sphere of commitment.

Next, you might like to indicate to yourself which items you wish to 'incubate' until some future time. These items go on the back burner until you are ready to give them more of your conscious attention. You may be familiar with the idea of 'sleeping on' a problem. While you sleep, your unconscious energy gets to work and when you wake, you know what you need to do. Incubating a project may mean putting it to one side until you feel clear to proceed with it and know what you have to do next.

Finally, you have your Activate items. In order to stay in conscious control of your life, make a list of these items separately, and alongside each your anticipated date of completion. If you have not handled an item by the date you set, you can always set a new date, or admit to yourself you are not going to do it, and eliminate the item from your conscious attention.

Your Activate list might look something like this:

Item	**Completion date**	
1. Mend the garage fuse	Sat'day	4 Mar
2. Finish watercolour painting	End of April	
3. Read/scan/discard stack of professional journals	Friday	16 Apr
4. Make dental appointment for kids	Today	27 Feb
5. Clear out attic		31 Mar
6. Repair dining table		15 Mar
7. Hire new assistant		7 Mar
8. Arrange dinner with Sid and Joan		27 Feb
9. Get the windows cleaned		3 Mar
10. Re-pot begonias		10 Mar

You might like to review your list, say once a week, to stay in touch with anything that is still outstanding, and enter additional items as they occur.

Clearing Out The Deadwood – Completion

Crossing items off your list will be one way of completing actions for yourself. In the process of clearing out the deadwood of the past, old friends or colleagues may come to mind and with them a sense of appreciation for whatever part they played in your life. You may wish to communicate something of your appreciation by letter or phone, or even just inwardly to yourself. Acts of appreciation are just another way of enhancing your experience of well-being.

Clearing out the deadwood is an approach which you may wish to adapt to suit your own circumstances more adequately.

*If you want
something new to happen
Make a space for it*

One of the most tangible forms of deadwood which can accumulate around us in home and office is that of our personal effects, clothing and papers for which we no longer have any use or value, but which have become almost 'invisible' to us. Clutter gathers around us unnoticed and may act as a screen to our clearest vision. There is often an association with the past attached to these objects. This is not necessarily bad, but if we are wanting to move ahead into a new, more rewarding lifestyle, memories of the past, connected with our environment, may hold us back.

For example, a person who is retiring no longer has the need of the business suits in his wardrobe. This brings to mind the example of the civil servant who, during his career, had all the grey dullness typically associated with civil servants. He did a nondescript clerical job from 9 to 4.30, wore grey, looked grey and had a grey personality. He retired early at 50.

A year after his retirement, he returned to visit his former colleagues, as a transformed person. Gone were the greys. He had grown his hair, wore a colourful silk cravat in an open-necked shirt and had taken up a career in portrait painting. He worked for six months of the year in a holiday camp, making enough to travel in the winter months. The sparkle of his personality matched his new-found freedom and pleasure in living.

Another example is that of a young woman who had for years written in journals of the pain she had experienced. She decided to discard and burn them all and her life subsequently took a distinct turn for the better. You might like to experiment, starting with one room at a time, emptying one drawer, or cupboard shelf, at a time and putting back only that which you really want. A refinement of this exercise is to put back only that which does not need any attention. So that if letters need answering, or clothing needs mending, a separate 'Action List' is created and those things are only returned to files, drawers and cupboards after the action is completed.

With anything you no longer need, you may decide to throw it away as rubbish, or give it away (such as clothing to the Salvation Army or a charity shop), or even sell it. You have probably heard stories of people who have discovered and sold antiques that were tucked away in a trunk, or even more common, people who hold a sale from the boot of their car, or garage, and raise unusually large sums of money from what they might have considered 'junk'.

A couple who cleared the clutter out of their modest Scottish home, and sold their unwanted items of household effects, raised £2,000, which they donated toward the relief of the Ethiopian famine.

Keeping our material effects in use and circulation can be seen to bring about financial well-being. If we tend to hold on to things just in case we might need them sometime, it reflects a 'needy' attitude and a fear of impoverishment. Clearing out deadwood is one way of healing that particular sense of insecurity.

There is also a connection between our freedom from clutter

and our good health. One family, three years after moving to their new home, still had packing cases lining the walls of their hallway and filling one spare room. They were suffering from congestive types of illness, chest infections and head colds. It was suggested to them that they unpack and clear out what they did not want. The congestion in their physical environment was having a negative influence on their health. They did clear out and sell a lot of their possessions, and their health improved. It was as though the improved circulation of their personal effects, and fresh space in their home was mirrored by the improved circulation within their physical bodies, producing better health.

Guidelines you might like to consider as you clear your physical environment are:

1. If there are objects you have not used for one year, other than things such as Christmas decorations you use only annually, you probably will not use them again, so discard them.

2. Clear only those objects for which you are directly responsible. Do not inflict your clearing out tendencies on your spouse or other family members if they are not willing to do their own clearing.

3. You may have old newspapers or documents or books that represent research material if you are a journalist, for example. Or you may have objects of genuine historical value to you. These would be stored in 'incubation'.

Clearing Out The Deadwood – Benefits

To summarize, the benefits you may experience from this exercise are any of the following:

1. Clarity of thinking, sense of purpose and direction
2. Ease in making positive changes in life
3. A wonderful feeling of liberation
4. Fresh creative inspiration

5. Increased inner motivation
6. Strengthened self-image
7. Improved health
8. Assertive and caring behaviour

As you reflect on (4), Completion, on the Action/Productivity Cycle you may not be familiar, or at all comfortable, with the idea of acknowledging and appreciating yourself. You may find that as you value and appreciate yourself more, others will reflect that attitude back to you in the ways they support and value you. Valuing yourself may enhance the quality of your personal relationships.

The following is an exercise in completion and is a way of reinforcing the sense of your own value.

A Letter of Appreciation
To Myself

For this exercise, it is important that you use the best quality of writing paper or personal letterhead as if you were writing to a potential employer, for example, or to someone you love and respect very much. Take some time to plan it so that you include all you might wish to say. This is only for your personal use and not for anyone else to read.

In the letter you do not express any self-recriminations, even the slightest denial, only appreciation and approval. Look out for the small details – sometimes, they are the ones that count the most. Decide the period of time you wish to cover – it could be a job that you are now leaving after three years; a household project that took you four months; a lifetime's career of 45 years; the completion of a four-year degree course. In a sense, you are writing your own 'Graduation Certificate' from the school of your life. Keep the tone of the letter warm and friendly.

Here are some points that you may wish to highlight:

- major accomplishments
- skills and abilities you developed
- challenges and obstacles you overcame
- lessons you learnt
- experiences which enriched you
- personal qualities and assets you noticed in yourself, and possibly developed (like patience, trust and self-confidence)
- contributions you made to yourself, your family, your community or the world around you
- gifts that you shared with others, material and otherwise

Conclude your letter with any words of encouragement and support that you would most like to give yourself for the future you are now moving into.

As a final touch to this exercise, write an envelope to yourself, seal your letter in it and put a postage stamp on it. Then ask a person you trust to mail it to you in two weeks' time. You may find that it comes into your hands at just the perfect moment!

You may wonder how these exercises could possibly have such a significant impact on the quality of your life. There is a subtle, yet powerful, process that happens each time we agree to fulfil a certain action or result, however small it seems. Our unconscious energy goes to work to assist in bringing about that outcome. If we fail to co-operate with our unconscious energy and attention by not taking physical action, then there is almost a sense of 'disappointment' or 'betrayal' felt within us. It is as if we have made an unspoken agreement with ourselves, and then broken it by not following through with it. In a hidden way, we hurt and let ourselves down.

An analogy might be that of telling a young child that you were going to buy an ice-cream and then you do not. The child might be angry and upset. You might think twice before agreeing to such a treat, unless you were really going to follow through with it. The unconscious within you will co-operate with you to a very high degree but less so when the 'agreements' that you undertake do not get fulfilled. Stage (2) of the Action/Productivity Cycle is where you can tidy up your outstanding commitments and regain inner harmony and control over your life.

Simplifying your life, taking on fewer commitments and only those which are important to you, will enhance your experience of successful living.

By taking action, as described in the previous exercises, the following blocks may be cleared:

1. Feelings of confusion
2. Fatigue and lethargy
3. Low self-confidence
4. Muddled thinking
5. Self-doubt
6. Lack of clarity and perspective
7. Poor motivation
8. Overwhelmed feelings and pressure
9. Misunderstandings
10. Stress

Of the three blocks illustrated in the Choice/Attitude Model (page 58), Deadwood is perhaps the most recognizable, tangible and easiest to clear. The blocks described as Comfort Zone and Self-Image on the Choice/Attitude Model are more in the nature of the inner or emotional resistance to change. Even though you are making clear and rational choices in favour of improving the quality of your life, there may be times when you feel held back in some way.

You may be like many of us who, while recognizing the appropriate action to take, nevertheless procrastinate, putting off doing anything about it. We sometimes label ourselves as being 'lazy'. This label may reflect a limiting aspect of our Self-Image.

Laziness may be nothing more than a lack of interest in what we have to do. You are probably not lazy about doing something that fully absorbs and interests you. A sense of being overwhelmed can also produce a feeling of laziness. The more we look at something we have to do, the more it seems to grow, and to build within us a resistance to taking the necessary action. So something small and easy to accomplish takes on extraordinary proportions in our minds and emotions as we put off doing it.

One approach to overcoming such hurdles is to find a first step towards resolving it that might take only two minutes. Then, having achieved that small step, find the next small step. And so on until you will probably find yourself getting involved and completing the whole task. For example, a small step might be making a phone call to get some necessary information, or finding the relevant folder from a filing cabinet. As the Chinese saying goes, a journey of a thousand miles starts with the first step.

To overcome lack of interest in some task you know you have to do, you may agree a small reward for yourself upon its completion, such as going for a walk, buying a magazine, reading the next chapter in a novel. It is important that you have the reward only when the action you have agreed to do is finished. Otherwise, you will be 'training' yourself into bad habits if you give in before you have 'earned' your reward.

The reluctance to move, or resistance to do what rationally you know you need to do, is an example of the emotional blocks we sometimes encounter in achieving what we want more of in life. For the most part, our emotional blocks are hidden within us, until such time as we want to do something, and then we may feel stuck, and wonder why.

One of the first reactions we may have when confronting one of these inner blocks is to criticize ourselves as being lazy, as in the example of procrastination, or greedy, when in fact we are feeling a sense of 'lack' or loss in our lives. Any accusation may seem to fit our particular incapacity of the moment but not be the most accurate description of what is happening within us. Such accusations will tend to trap us within the block even more and make it harder to act. It is rather like finding ourselves guilty, then putting ourselves in a prison of limiting self-image.

In many cultures, children are brought up with punishment as a motivation to do better. These children grow up having learnt the habit within themselves of punishing themselves for their 'failures', instead of rewarding themselves for their successes. In terms of inner motivation, and their personal well-being and vitality, this would be like being beaten back three steps for every one taken forward. This is a waste of precious energy. It may not be necessary to feel the pain of self-imposed discouragement on the way to achieving what you want out of your life. You may recognize this pattern in yourself.

A kinder approach is to simply acknowledge and accept your emotional block, without condemning yourself for encountering it. That acceptance may in itself be a major hurdle. Once you have accepted the limiting or negative emotion within you, then you become available first of all to the information, or awareness it holds for you. Then, spontaneously you may more easily get in touch with the next simple action you need to take to switch the limiting energy into a positive resource. As you take the necessary action, the block dissolves itself.

The next exercise is useful for simply observing your negative feelings, noticing if there is some information for you in them and finally choosing some action to take. Physical action is one of the best remedies for negative emotion. It is harder to be depressed when you are running, or swimming, for example.

The 3 'A' Steps For Overcoming Emotional Blocks

These three steps are statements that you can repeat within yourself when you find yourself stuck with any negative emotion. That could include anger, resentment, guilt, fear, depression. You may wish to repeat the three steps over more than once until you determine some action you will take to move beyond what was previously limiting you. The best way to do the exercise is to begin the statement and allow yourself to complete it spontaneously with whatever pops into mind.

1. Acceptance

First accept your negative mood or emotion. The statement begins:
   I accept that . . .

2. Awareness

A negative mood may be rich with information for us and blesses us with a gift, if we can stand back and observe it with some detachment. This statement begins:
   I am aware that . . .

3. Action

However negative we may have been feeling, emotion, seen objectively, is only a build up of energy within us. If we can find a suitable outlet or channel for that energy, we can effectively disperse it and feel better.
   Having gained some information, or awareness, of your emotional block, then begin the next statement:
   My action is to . . .

The following examples illustrate how this exercise may look:

- I accept that I feel angry.
- I am aware that I sometimes feel angry when I feel other people are not doing things the best way I think they should be done.
- My action is to come up with a constructive alternative solution that may help us to complete the project.

- I accept that I feel depressed.
- I am aware that I am expecting too much of myself as being the perfect mother.
- My action is to ease up on myself and repeat this exercise.
- I accept that I feel depressed.
- I am aware that I am a good mother in many ways.
- My action is to tell Sarah how much I love and appreciate her just the way she is.

- I accept that my shoulders are aching right now.
- I am aware that I am trying to do too much today.
- My action is to relax and have a break for 15 minutes when I have completed this particular task.

- I accept that I am concerned about my finances.
- I am aware that I have been putting off talking to my bank manager and have not yet worked out my budget for the month.
- My action is to make an appointment with the bank manager and set aside 2 hours to work out my budget.
- I accept that I am worried about money.
- I am aware that I usually have enough for my needs.
- My action is to make a list of the money I am currently owing, and make a plan to pay off my debts.

- I accept that I am scared of making the presentation.
- I am aware that the service I have to offer is really good.
- My action is to re-read through all the letters of appreciation and acknowledgement I have received and re-build my confidence.

Your Comfort Zone embraces your familiar habits, routines, set patterns and ways of doing things, your expectations about the way life is for you. Unconsciously, much of your life may have been 'on automatic' so that you got up at a certain time, dressed a certain way, took the same route to work, met the same people, went to the same club in the evening and so on. In one sense, you might have been 'in a rut' and so changing any aspect of your pattern of life can be exciting as you view life in new ways. Making such changes is a challenge to your personal level of vitality and can provide welcome stimulation.

There may be times when such challenges are almost too scary for you. You may feel shaken, or troubled with feelings of anxiety towards what the future is bringing for you, or a fear of the 'unknown'. Your Comfort Zone also tends to be reinforced by people around you who are accustomed to the various aspects of your lifestyle, including how you relate with these people. As you begin to change your patterns of living, it challenges the Comfort Zones of those around you. They may feel shaken by your new outlook and react to try to get you to 'conform' to the former you that they know and feel safe with. The people closest to you may need the reassurance that you still love and care for them.

Similarly, your Self-Image may be challenged by the new vision or set of objectives you have chosen. For example, you may have clearly chosen a new quality or experience in your life, but underneath doubt that you are worth having it. The blocks relating to your Self-Image concern your attitudes and beliefs about yourself and the sense of your personal boundaries or limitations. Given your former set of conditions and experience in life, your Self-Image may have been quite 'accurate'. The emotional resistance you may encounter could include a sense of personal inadequacy, discouragement and feelings of self-doubt or self-rejection.

In *Set Personal Objectives*, you were looking at goals in three sections. The first section was the one relating to your own most personal goals, those over which you have greatest potential control and accountability. It is these that will perhaps demand your greatest self-discipline and strength and most challenge your existing Self-Image. In *Create Inner Strength*, we shall be exploring ways in which you can re-build your self-image to enhance your experience of success. Refocusing on the experiences you are wanting more of within yourself is one of the best ways of clearing the emotional blocks that come from the area of Self-Image. In a sense, what you can do is create within you a new experience of who you are.

To illustrate this idea, as you progress towards your set of objectives you may encounter some limiting belief about yourself. As this knowledge comes to light, you become aware of a weakness that you can address constructively by finding the strength or quality within yourself to overcome it.

In a similar way, your Comfort Zone, which governs the familiar patterns and routines of your life, will throw up emotional blocks as you enter unfamiliar territory for the first time. The Comfort Zone acts like a self-regulating mechanism, such as a thermostat, which keeps you in order. This is useful in that when you want to change the 'order', it serves you by holding you in restraint until the order you are now choosing is one that you really do want. If you fight the block it presents to you, you may feel very frustrated. Have you ever found yourself wanting to move ahead and feeling cross with yourself because things are not moving as fast as you would like?

The best course with any block is first of all to relax and accept it, and not fight it. Then, having first accepted and observed it for what it is, find the next best action to take. What if all the blocks and obstacles we encounter exist to serve us? What if there is a way that things work out for us, a sense of purpose and timing relating to our progress through life? When you are selective and clear about the choices you are making in your life, you will find adequate resources appropriate to your needs, in terms of time, money, people or any other assets, in order to move towards a successful lifestyle.

In *Expect Success*, you will be able to create the experience within yourself of your new preferred Comfort Zone. By using your imagination, you can bring your mind and emotions to entertain and become comfortable with the new set of circumstances that you are now choosing for yourself. This is a way of re-programming your self-regulating mechanism. It is also another method of assisting you to focus positively on what you want more of in your life, on whatever successful living is for you.

Looking at the Choice/Attitude Model, the more you can amplify your direction forward, the less the limitations of the past can exercise a hold over you.

There may be times when your feelings of frustration, doubt, anxiety or fear, for example, are too strong for you to be able to relax and listen to the information they are giving. One of the best, simplest and most effective ways for clearing the block of negative emotions is to write out exactly how you are feeling in a spontaneous and 'free form' way.

Write – And Release Yourself From Your Emotional Blocks

Set aside for yourself a time and place to be undisturbed or distracted by any other needs or commitments. Take a pad of paper and a ball-point pen (you may want to write forcibly and a pencil or fountain pen may not take the pressure). Now write out spontaneously any thought or feeling that pops into your mind. If you are angry, write out that anger, turn the page blue if you want to. In the process of doing this, you may find old hurts and upsets surfacing. If tears start to come, let them flow, and keep writing out the disappointments, misunderstandings and pain – the paper will not mind or criticize you for your feelings. Give yourself permission to express yourself freely like you never have before. Whatever the negative emotion, get it out of you, and on to the paper. If your thoughts seem to tumble out of you, faster than you can write, don't worry if your sentences are incomplete, or words are misspelled. Just keep going with the exercise until you feel clear, relaxed and peaceful.

Then, *on no account read anything you have written*. Let it go and forget it. Find a safe place to burn that paper, shred it, or flush it down the toilet.

This is a wonderful exercise to do when your confusion is at its height. Done regularly every so often for perhaps 10 minutes at a time, you may discover some very valuable and inspired thoughts coming 'from out of the blue'. Allow yourself to be very spontaneous and watch what happens!

Sometimes, the blocks we meet in working towards a goal seem to have more to do with other people than with ourselves. Others are sometimes less than co-operative with our plans. The challenge here may be in our communications with others. Clear communications with others begin with a clear line of communication with your own inner knowledge, feelings and responses as you interact with the world around you. Have you ever found yourself in a situation and had a sixth sense that something was not quite as it should be for you in some way? An inner voice seems to be calling us, and it is useful to pay attention to what it has to say.

If other people seem to be standing in your way, notice what they may be presenting to you in the way of information so that you can move even more freely ahead.

When you are feeling blocked within a relationship, you have basically two choices. You can stay with it and make changes within yourself, to bring about harmony and fulfilment, no matter what the external conditions are. This is a choice that can bring tremendous personal strength and freedom because finally any relationship you have reflects something of the relationship with yourself.

However, there are times when an existing relationship or

partnership really does not serve you. Then you must leave it, with as much grace and goodwill as possible. Either way, if you can hold within you the greatest respect and appreciation possible for the other person or people involved, it will significantly ease the release of the obstacles they are apparently causing.

Only you will know, deep down, when a relationship is over, or complete for you. The fear of losing friend or lover, a fear of the emotions of grief, could stand in the way of letting go of what no longer supports you, and your freedom and vitality. It could be a rebelliousness, or reluctance to change your attitudes and patterns of behaviour, that could block you from fulfilment within a partnership. One way or another, being clear about what you want, inwardly first of all, is your first challenge. Know yourself; be true to yourself; above all, be loving to yourself. This will assist you to be more loving in your partnerships. A caring, considerate attitude towards yourself and others makes for success in personal relationships.

This next exercise will help you to become clearer about any partnership with which you are experiencing some doubt. This could be a personal or working relationship. Even if you cannot express yourself clearly to another person, be very honest with yourself in discovering what is true for you.

Be Clear With Those You Love And Care For

For this exercise you will need pen and paper. Bring the name of the person concerned to mind and write their name down in block capitals at the head of the paper.

Notice any emotional reaction that surfaces with their name, and write down your responses. For example: fear, love, sadness, longing, anger etc.

Reflect on the circumstances of your relationship with the person. In which situations do you have a positive experience; which produce conflict for you? Divide the page into columns with your positive responses in one column and the negative in the other column. So the page might look like this:

POSITIVE	NEGATIVE
We spark off good ideas in problem-solving situations	She is slow to grasp the most obvious points in our Board meetings
We are both inspired by the project	Her lack of dress sense lets us both down when we are meeting clients

Etc.

OR

He is a wonderful father to our children	He can't keep his eyes off other women when we go out
We have a great time when we are on holiday as a family	He works late most evenings and I never know when he is going to be back for dinner

Etc.

Take plenty of time to surface all the 'considerations' that make up the block, so that instead of having a chaos of mixed emotions swimming around in your head, you at least have some facts to observe. If the negatives far outweigh your positives, you have either a rich opportunity for self-development and growth, or a clear picture of why you want to end the relationship in its present form! With clarity, it becomes easier to choose wisely.

In either event, take a clean sheet of paper, and write out all the positives, starting each statement:

I am grateful for . . .

and put that to one side.

The negatives, which are your experience, now come into the realm of your personal accountability or responsibility. These reflect your perception and therefore you have the power to effect a new choice, a *change of experience* within you.

The first possibility is that you come to know within you that you no longer wish to participate in the relationship. So, for the purposes of this exercise, when you have completed your 'I am grateful . . .' statements, destroy the first sheet of paper. Your 'I am grateful . . .' statements will make it easier to release yourself from the partnership.

If you choose to continue, and effect some positive changes, take each 'negative' point one by one and with a positive regard for both yourself and the other person, look at your options.

Once you have clarified your view, the greatest challenge here is to communicate your needs, and suggestions for improvement, clearly to the other person, without degenerating into dissension and blame. Be very aware that the criticisms you have been levelling at someone else may be a projection of some area of your own sense of inadequacy. Remember, you have much greater control over your own performance than you will ever have over anyone else's. Try to change others, and you may end up feeling very blocked indeed!

If the people to whom you are close seem to get in your way at times, they can also be one of your best resources for problem solving and releasing you from your blocks. It is not always those closest to you that can assist you because they may be too closely involved with the block concerned. You may find it helpful to seek the counsel of one or more others who can help you to listen to yourself more clearly.

The best person, or group of people, to approach are those who are able to be objective as they listen and suggest ways forward. Let them offer you many options from which you can choose, rather than one course of action you feel you must follow. Beware of following someone else's advice unthinkingly, and then finding yourself blaming them if your actions do not produce a positive outcome for yourself.

The next exercise illustrates an open-minded approach to clearing away a block.

Problem Solving with the Angel's Advocate

The purpose of this exercise is to open doors and keep options flowing until a clear solution presents itself.

The first step is for you, as the person concerned, to present the problem or issue as it stands.

Another person, or yourself acting as the Angel's Advocate, offers a suggestion about how to resolve it.

You must find something about the suggestion with which you can agree. Then you can add your own creative possibility, not necessarily the action you will finally take. In this way, you keep an open channel for new ideas to flow through. So instead of saying:

'That would never work for me because . . .', the response would be more like:

'What I like about that is . . ., and the way it could work for me is . . .'

In a group situation, several suggestions offered and worked in this way will provide you with steps required for solution. You, as the individual who is finally responsible for the issue, will have the final say and act accordingly.

What you must prevent at all costs is generating new blocks, or any other discouragement, into the discussion. This is a process of expansion. Keep doors opening and monitor any inclination to contract, or sabotage any suggestions with criticisms. You may find it helpful to write up each idea on a sheet of paper, visible to everyone if you are doing this with others.

You, as caretaker of the issue, have the total picture available to you, and the resource of other people, positively directed, will facilitate the release of the block. The creative presentation of possible solutions is very like peeling off the layers of an onion until you get to the centre and the answers that you have stored within you.

An emotional block you might experience in moving towards your goals is that of 'lack', or possibly, more accurately, the feeling of lack. As you let go of the old, there is sometimes a feeling of loss. Until you have arrived at your new lifestyle, you may be aware of a gap.

The feeling of lack, or emptiness, inside you may be projected outwards into the material world around you, including your financial resources. You seem to notice shortages, not only in your personal world, but in the world as a whole. Yet the truth is that the world is full of excesses. You can probably identify places where there is too much money, too much rain, too much sun, too much food, for example.

With a personal fear of lack is the concern that there is not enough of what you consider you need for your survival. This sense of lack could well concern your perception, rather than the reality of your circumstances.

For example, the wife of a bank manager approaching retirement found that she woke in the night with panic attacks about there not being enough money for their retirement, even though they were well provided for. Fears concerning money are typically more acute *before* the retirement date.

Once a couple has entered retirement, they usually learn how to manage their financial resources with a degree of confidence. The longer-term difficulty has usually to do with finding an outlet for contributing something of value, finding a way of giving of themselves to regain a sense of self-esteem. Your feeling of lack may have less to do with what you have, and more to do with what you are not giving. Find a way of giving, and the feeling of 'lack' disappears with it.

Sometimes, no matter how much we have to enjoy materially, we remain driven to fill the emptiness we feel inside. This can be done by eating or drinking in excess of our physical needs, or with other forms of mental and emotional stimulation, but none of these bring about the quality of inner success and well-being.

Paradoxically, perhaps, we become fulfilled, and inwardly successful, as we give out, not as we take in.

When supply seems to have failed,
you must know that it has not done so.

But you must look round
to see what you can give away.

Give away something.

There are three principles for addressing and releasing the feelings of fear, and emotional limitation and contraction, associated with 'lack'.

1. Keep Your Financial House In Order

Put simply: you must know what you have, what you may owe, what arrangements you need to make to repay any money you owe in small, manageable stages. Communicate with those to whom you owe money, and have the courage to put them in the picture. Also be aware of the money owing to you, from any source. Maintain a record of your material assets. Failure to know what you do have may cause you to feel a lack unnecessarily.

If you are getting into trouble because you are living beyond your means, such as living a champagne lifestyle on a beer income, look into how you can both increase your income and decrease your expenses. Money itself is a matter of common sense, but the emotions you attach to it obscure the business of managing it well.

Know and record also the sum total of your assets, in material worth and personal, inner resources. These you may recall from the Taking Stock exercise in *Set Personal Objectives*. Information can be a great antidote for anxiety.

2. Be Giving of Yourself

It does not really matter what you give, or where you give. You could give of your time to assist others. Speak kindly to others and offer encouragement. Or give of your money, or any personal resource that you have available. Perhaps what matters more is how you give. If you can give for the joy of giving, without expecting anything in return, the inner rewards are very great. If there is any sense of disappointment in your giving, then you might have attached some importance to receiving a positive response, acknowledgement or praise. You might like to experiment one day and find a large number of small ways you can give of yourself, and notice how you feel at the end of the day.

Financially, you might experiment with leaving a larger tip than usual, anonymously giving money and other gifts, leaving small change in telephone booths or ticket machines, paying for the next five cars in line for a tollbooth, buying theatre tickets and sending them anonymously to a friend. Find small ways of giving money to begin with and notice how much freer you feel towards money as a resource in your life.

You could look for ways of giving your time, voluntarily. If you are unemployed, in the process of applying for a new job, with some time on your hands, look for where you can give a few hours a week to a local charity. Do whatever you can to open the channels of giving, freely and happily. Give where you know you can give with the greatest joy. Get physically active, and observe your new enthusiasm for life releasing old blocks.

3. Value Yourself and Be Open to Receiving

When you recognize the benefits of giving, you may also recognize the value in allowing yourself to receive from others. Sometimes when we have a need, we make it worse by refusing to ask for assistance. It is a kind act to ask others for their assistance because it facilitates their opportunity for giving. People, at heart, are givers. It is through their giving, and the expression of their caring, that they also gain fulfilment.

If you are inclined to deny or reject yourself, you may just not feel a good enough person, worthy to receive from others, whether it is friends, support, achievement, fulfilment, even the success you most want. There are two emotional attitudes that block the value we hold towards ourselves and make us feel less than worthwhile, less than worthy of receiving from others. These are resentment (an emotion directed against others) and guilt (an emotion directed inwardly against ourselves).

A forgiving attitude releases the blocks of both resentment and guilt. The lack of forgiveness blocks your capacity for receiving all your potential success.

When you have a forgiving attitude towards yourself, valuing yourself enough to have what you want, you also release the resentment towards others. It is curious that often what we see and resent in others reflects something we cannot accept within ourselves. Thus, as you forgive others, you also release a block to the experience of your own well-being.

If you want to enjoy and make the most of the present, cut away the hurts of the past and allow yourself to move more freely forward. Forgive yourself and others for all the misunderstandings, rejections, disappointments, hurt feelings and disturbances that you have experienced and notice how the quality of your life improves.

There is a simple exercise you can do at night before going to sleep. It only takes a few minutes. Your experiences of forgiving and gratitude will lift your perception of yourself, your sense of worth and openness to receive.

I Forgive . . . I am Grateful For . . .

Write the sentence starters above on a pad or piece of paper and leave it somewhere so that you will see it last thing at night before turning the light off. Reflect back over the day and as many times as you need, complete the sentence in your mind:

I forgive . . . as any thoughts or incidents occur to you
For example:

I forgive Mum for shouting at me.
I forgive myself for being late arriving at work.
I forgive the terrorist who planted that bomb today.
I forgive God for the problems in our world.
I forgive myself for criticizing the things I said.
Etc.

Similarly, reflect back over the day and begin to count all that happened for which you were grateful, completing the sentence:

I am grateful for . . .
and repeat that as you count the blessings of the day.
For example:

I am grateful for talking with Diana today.
I am grateful for the sunshine.
I am grateful for my walk.
I am grateful for the support I received.
I am grateful for my home.
Etc.

This exercise will assist you in clearing away any blocks of the day, releasing you into a good night's sleep and a fresh start in the morning. Let the morning begin with a clear, open view of the day free for new opportunities.

The relationship we have with any aspect of our outer world reflects the relationship we have within ourselves. In order to fill ourselves with an experience of success, we can begin by releasing any inner blocks that we have held against ourselves. Sometimes, we find it easier to forgive others for their weaknesses and are much more demanding of ourselves. In this next guided visualization, breathe in fully the quality of forgiveness towards yourself.

Forgiving Yourself

For this guided visualization, choose a time and place in which you will be free and undisturbed to nurture a refreshing new vision for yourself. Feel free to put it onto a cassette tape so that you can sit back comfortably and follow through the images with your eyes closed. Remember, if you do this, to allow spaces in your recording for the images to come forward in your mind.

Begin by taking in a deep breath . . . exhaling and letting go of any tensions, aches or stresses in your physical body . . . Breathe in again, this time breathing in a deep relaxation . . . Exhale and let go of any tired old emotions, upsets, concerns, anxieties . . . Once again, breathe in deeply . . . and this time, breathe in a peacefulness . . . fill yourself with this peace and quiet . . . Exhale . . . and feel the peace within you expand and fill every cell of your body . . .

Bring to your mind anything you would consider to be a block in your life . . . It could be an attitude . . . Another person . . . A situation which seems stuck . . . A problem . . . What does it look like? . . . How does it feel for you? . . . How does it sound to you? . . . What have you judged about this block? . . . How is it wrong in your eyes? . . . Is there something about yourself that you are seeing as wrong . . . or bad, in some way? . . . What have you told yourself . . . or others . . . about this block? . . .

What is this block preventing you from having . . . or doing . . . or being? . . . Bring to mind now the picture of what it is that you want more . . . more than the block of limitation . . . It could be more money . . . a fulfilling marriage . . . a rewarding career . . . a baby . . . a university degree . . . successful business . . . Envisage in vivid detail your new choice . . . most of all experience the fullness of it . . . the gratitude for having this new gift in your life . . . Breathe it in deeply and expand it . . .

Review the block . . . now with the quality of life . . . the inner abundance . . . of having fulfilled your dream . . . Observe in detachment the negative labels . . . the former judgements . . . you gave to the old condition . . . One by one, take each judgement and say to yourself . . . I forgive myself . . . or I forgive the other person . . . until you have released all the grains of sand in that old block . . .

Receive the freedom, the exhilaration of your forgiving . . . Breathe it in . . . Expand it . . . enjoy your release into a new dimension of living . . .

Now . . . very gradually . . . maintaining contact with the good feelings inside you . . . bring yourself back into your room, feeling clearer and more refreshed than ever before.

With any block you encounter, you always have the choice to be constructively a part of the solution. Whatever the block experienced in the course of moving forward in your life, there is one attitude that can assist you in overcoming it. No matter how challenging and difficult progress may seem to be, remember that:

Enough loving heals all things.

As you are the primary source of your solutions, this caring attitude begins with yourself.

Chapter 4

Create Inner Strength

Your greatest lifetime resource is your inner self. You are the one that will make the changes and create what you want in life. At times, this seems easier said than done. So in order to gain maximum satisfaction from your endeavours, strengthening your inner resolve will prove to be important.

In *Set Personal Objectives,* there were three areas for setting goals. The first, in which you have greatest control and direction, is that of: **Health/Fitness; Personal Philosophy; Spiritual/Religious.** If you have not yet clarified objectives for yourself this area, this chapter may assist you to get in touch with your deeper motives.

In one sense, you already have inner strength and have no need to create it. If you could begin to imagine all the obstacles there are in the world to our being healthy, it is impressive how many of us are resilient and so well. However, what you may create is the attunement with the inner strength which already exists within you. This would mean first recognizing, accepting and appreciating the strength that you have, and then taking action to enhance it.

You may have felt that success would come easily, if only the world around you did not present so many obstacles to it. It might be pleasant to imagine a world in which there was no disease, no stress, no conflicts or troubles of any kind. Yet given the circumstances in which we find ourselves, perhaps there is a great benefit for us to be challenged constantly to seek, find and create the improvements we would like.

Perhaps it is hard for you to believe that you can always choose how you feel inside, even when the outer circumstances are unpleasant. For example, if someone were shouting angrily at you, how could you be peaceful inside? If you were to watch the news on TV, and saw murder, famine or war being reported, how could you feel happy? If your home were burgled, how could you be relaxed? There is a moment of impact with these kinds of situation when you do feel a negative response within you. However, you do have a choice about whether you promote and prolong the negative feelings, or switch your attention into something more lifting, expansive and positive.

It has been said that the mind can only hold one thought at a time. In each moment, two different thoughts cannot co-exist in the mind. One thought can follow another very quickly, so they may seem to co-exist, but in fact they do not. Think for a moment about your left big toe. Now think about your right elbow. Now think about your nose. When you are thinking about your nose, what happened to your thought about your big toe?

So, if you are intent on sadness and depression, you exclude the possibility of happiness. With care, attention and practice, you can train yourself to maintain an intent of happiness. This is rather like developing an inner muscle for relaxing you out of the negative and into the positive. It does not mean that you will never feel sad or depressed ever again. Those negative responses are important and valuable to you, if only to alert you. However, if you are actively involved in strengthening the positive, it is easier to confront and release the negatives when they strike.

Switch To The Positive

This exercise demonstrates the control you have over your inner environment. First of all, bring to your mind a time from the past when things did not go well for you. You made some mistakes and experienced a failure of some kind. What were some of the negative things you felt about yourself, or told yourself? As you bring this situation or event to mind, notice how you feel now. Are you a little sad or disappointed? Do you feel even a bit low? Do you notice any aches or tensions appearing in your body? You might even notice your body sagging, or drooping a bit.

Now take in a few really deep breaths, as you do so, fill yourself with fresh energy. Stand up and stretch your muscles. Look around you for an object, a word, something that has a strength, a positive quality to it. What is that positive quality you notice? Breathe deeply again, and let yourself relax.

For example, you might notice an orange on a plate. What is the positive quality that you notice? It has a vivid, sustaining colour. Sustaining or endurance would be the quality.

Bring the three most positive qualities you can think of to mind. What are they? Write them down somewhere in large, block capitals, in a colour if you like. Take each quality one by one, and breathe the quality in to you. If it were happiness, envisage happiness bubbling through your bloodstream, through all your veins and arteries, into every cell of your body, so that all your bones, skin, heart, liver and every organ is filled with happiness. How are you feeling now?

You may have observed that while you were engaged in entertaining the positive qualities, you were no longer aware of the former negative memory from the past.

If there is any situation that keeps surfacing a specific negative feeling, you can use this exercise to sow the seeds of a new set of conditions for yourself. Supposing you kept feeling doubt, for example. Even though rationally you are set on course and clear about your goals, nevertheless emotionally you feel shaky and unsure.

What would you prefer to feel? Say that you would rather feel confidence. First of all, bring to mind an occasion when you experienced confidence. Picture the circumstances in detail so that you once again become fully involved in that experience of confidence. Now do the breathing exercise with confidence as your theme. As the quality of confidence is finding its way more deeply and fully throughout you, allow any new images, sounds and other associated feelings to come to mind. You can make a note of them as they appear.

In times of stress, when doubt reappears, take three deep breaths and re-awaken yourself to your images and feelings of confidence. This is not an exercise to be mastered fully in one go. It will take time, persistence and patience to strengthen yourself in the new quality. As you do however, you will probably notice how the world begins to respond better to you.

As a note of appreciation, thank yourself for having this new quality more vibrantly alive within you. Feelings of gratitude are one way of making sure your new quality holds strong within you.

If you look back to the Choice/Attitude Model from *Unlock Your Attitude*, you will notice on the centre vertical line, the words Now, Choice and Turning Point. It is this choice, in each moment now, that will be instrumental in creating your inner strength.

What you need to do is prepare your inner environment in such a way that you can, as easily as possible, switch from negative to positive when presented with a challenge. You can also ask those around you to support you in your ability to keep returning to the positive. Create your living and working spaces to assist you in feeling good about who you are. This might involve cleaning, re-decorating or changing furniture.

Probably in the course of growing up you have been 'educated', as much by experience as anything else, to undervalue yourself in some capacity, and deep down, doubt that you are worth having the success you want. This belief has very likely been reinforced by your subsequent behaviour and actions.

Take the time now to switch channels and begin to value who you are, in spite of all your mistakes, faults and lack of what you consider a good human being should be, have or do. Moving into your positive outlets for success is challenging, particularly where the limitations have had a subtle, well-hidden hold on you. It will take some fun, even dramatic and highly imaginative methods to make the switch effectively, and it may even be a lifetime process for many of us. The route of entertainment and laughter is one which will most easily distract you from the lesser experiences, and facilitate the greatest relaxation, openness, learning and the maximum movement forward.

A resource all human beings have potentially is to maintain humour in the worst of circumstances. You can either distance yourself in time from a 'disaster' to see the funny side of it, or you can lift yourself above it, at the time it happens, to see the funny side. After all, if it is to be funny later, why not see it as funny now so that you can free yourself now to move ahead? This may seem impossible, but how much easier life would become if we could keep a light touch in our heavier moments.

Perhaps the cause for celebration is also an opportunity for enjoyment and fun. At the point of completion (4) of the Action/Productivity Cycle, we not only fully release ourselves from the past but in acknowledging and celebrating our strengths, we make them more fully available to us for our new goals.

Celebrating Your Wins!

This exercise is one to free you more completely to move ahead and into your objectives. First of all, you need to choose the period of time on which you will reflect and note your wins. It could be the past year within a career where you are now moving into a promotion; or it could be 15 years of being within a corporate environment, and you are now establishing your own business venture; or you might be concluding a period, say eight years, of having had several close relationships, and are now wanting to be married; or, you may have been married for six years, and are now wanting to start a family. These would all be circumstances of change in which you want to experience greater emotional and/or material fulfilment.

Reflect back over your chosen period of time in detail and with a pen and paper, make notes of all your wins. There may have been times when you were personally challenged and brought forward a quality which progressed an aim. In a relationship, there may have been times when instead of giving in to anger or depression, you turned to the loving wisdom within you and transformed a situation.

Only record those actions, thoughts and behaviours which were 100 per cent *wins* for you. For the purpose of this exercise, do not credit others for the win. Recognize yourself as the winner in each event. Accountability does not only mean that you are accountable when things go badly. Accountability also embraces your successes, so give yourself that credit where credit is due.

When you have completed the first part of the exercise, and have thoroughly brought to paper *all* your wins for the period of time you chose, now brainstorm some possible rewards and celebrations that will most vividly demonstrate to yourself that you are a *winner*. This can involve others, but not necessarily. Your choice need not be expensive. Let your imagination play a role here. Make it something unusual, something you would not normally do for yourself, or ask for yourself, such as a special journey, party, trip to the theatre, for example. If nothing comes to mind instantly, sleep on it, and be prepared on waking to get an idea.

When you have chosen your celebration, make time in your diary to carry it out. This exercise is not complete until you take action. Thinking about it is definitely not enough. And have fun!

Value yourself, and your world (particularly the people in it) will value you, and pay their respects in many ways. This is an important part of being true to yourself and the strengths within you, with which you were born. In order to stay within the sense of your own value, you may need to train yourself to keep in touch with and aware of it. The discipline of maintaining a strong self-image in this way will give you increased energy for meeting your new objectives.

Here is an experiment that may interest you. When you are next in a large group of people, or in a public place of some kind, tell yourself to look for the colour red, and notice how your eyes are drawn to many red objects in your view. You could experiment with different colours. Look for a colour, and you will find a colour. Look for sadness, and you will find sadness. Look for good, and you will find good. What you look for is what you will see. The starting point in this experiment is choosing the object for your vision.

Maintaining a positive and constructive outlook in your life takes watchfulness and then self-discipline. You need to be aware of the times that you get pulled back into a negative perspective. Notice when you are tired, hungry, bored or stressed in some way. Then it is important that you take care of your basic needs so that you can view life afresh. Pushing too hard on yourself will not pay off in the longer term. The fundamental essentials of adequate sleep, balanced diet and some form of regular physical exercise are important ingredients of a successful life. If you are denying yourself the basic needs of life, how can you enjoy to the full your greatest success?

Caring self-discipline will increase your self-esteem, your self-image and capacity for having more wins in the future.

Your Body Plan

Building your inner strength will be enhanced by a fitter physical body. The discipline that you exercise towards your body will promote your inner strength.

If you are going to set any plan for better health, make sure that you are not over-ambitious. The best way is to start with some small adjustments to your regular routine or habits; benefit from the improvement and make another small adjustment. For example, dieting is sometimes fraught with failure because the measures recommended are too extreme, and difficult to incorporate into a working life.

Begin by reviewing the areas of:

- Exercise
- Eating habits
- Sleep

Physical exercise will promote your suppleness, strength and/or stamina. Choose a form of exercise that is enjoyable for you, something you can look forward to doing, rather than a 'punishment' about which you will feel good only after you have done it. Walking and swimming have many benefits. Or you may prefer something more energetic, such as running, tennis or aerobics. How much time in the week can you reasonably give to this exercise? If it is only 10 minutes three times a week, that may be a good start.

There is increasing information available on the foods we should be eating, and there are often fads. Fibre is one that has been popular for a while, although fibre by itself is not enough: it must be accompanied by plenty of water to have its desired effect of eliminating toxins from the body. How can you improve your nutrition? What foods do you know are best for you? Is there anything that you eat too much of, or too little? Do you give enough time and thought to your food? Or do you grab snacks in the course of a busy day? Is your body weight acceptable to you? What small adjustments can you begin to introduce to yourself to improve your nutrition?

If you do not already know it, you might like to experiment and find out which foods your body best digests and utilizes. You may function well on a high-carbohydrate diet; or dairy-based foods; or very low fat. It is important to have a balance of the following 7 nutrients:

- vitamins
- minerals
- fats
- carbohydrates
- salt
- fibre
- water

If you are looking to reduce weight, make a small goal to begin with and possibly have an ideal weight to aim for in the longer term. Stay loving and flexible towards yourself as you work with your body weight.

As with exercise, choose the most enjoyable foods for you. Choose the balance and variety of foods which have colour and appeal. Look for the value in, and appreciate, your body for how it serves you, no matter what your weight.

Sleep: are you getting enough rest and relaxation? If you eat and drink too many stimulants you may have difficulty sleeping well. Watching TV news or doing crosswords last thing at night may not make for a peaceful mind. Do you 'need' a drink to sleep at night, or drug of some kind? Do you need to sleep longer at night? Or just improve the quality of your sleep? What can you do to be more relaxed and rested, open and receptive during the course of your daily life?

Incorporate your Body Plan into your life in small achievable steps, and notice how you begin to feel better about yourself as you do.

Learning to be true to yourself and your needs is going to contribute to your inner strength. Have you in the past been 'true' to yourself more out of stubbornness, rebellion and anger? Or have you noticed yourself being pushed around by what others wanted of you, or you thought others wanted of you? Or have you been trying to uphold a romantic ideal of some kind, a perfect image, which does not reflect your most deeply-felt concerns?

As you move forward into the truer picture of yourself and your success, you will need to make changes not only to your inner environment, but your outer one as well, so that it represents the new picture of you. This comes close to clearing out the deadwood, but it is more subtle. For example, you may have a tendency to hold on to your romantic memories and mementoes of the past, with their hidden hurts. Notice whether these objects will contribute an active part of your new successful lifestyle.

For example, you may wish to enjoy a fulfilling marriage and yet retain photos and letters from former relationships which were perhaps less than satisfactory, but now have a sentimental glow. There may be a safety, and familiarity, in retaining the sentiment from the past. In that case, you risk not being fully available to enjoy a new, potentially more fulfilling, experience in the present, and perhaps not getting it.

Retaining memories of either the pain or pleasures of the past is a subtle way of blocking your new vision from becoming real. If you are holding on to souvenirs, or are continuing limiting behaviours and habits that do not reflect the new kind of marriage or relationship experience you want, you will be standing in your own way.

For example, if you wish to experience a successful marriage, spend some of your time with friends who are happily married for new role models, or living examples of what you want. You might spend less time trying to find that relationship, alone in bars and discotheques where single people perhaps seek entertainment for the evening. Once you 'fly in your own true colours', actively engaged and absorbed in those pursuits which bring you most fulfilment, you stand a better chance of attracting to you a like-minded person with whom you can enjoy a successful partnership.

If you are wanting more financial wealth, notice what you have around you that reflects fears or concerns about 'poverty'. Do you hoard paper clips, for example, or any other small, simple resource for fear of not being able to get any more? Real wealth may have more to do with what you can live without, rather than what you think you might need. Wealth might be spelt 'wellth', meaning well-being, and reflect more accurately your goal. Build your inner strength by noticing and letting go of what you do not need as part of your fuller picture of success.

Know Yourself – Be True to Yourself

This is an exercise for you to discover how you feel differently as you become truer to yourself.

First of all, reflect on some of the things you feel *obliged* to do, particularly those that are perhaps not essential. There may be people you think you should spend time with for some reason, but whom you do not really like very much. Or you may be doing some charitable task, but not with a lot of pleasure. Bring some examples to mind and with each, complete the following sentences:

'I don't have to . . .'

'And if I want to . . ., I can.'

This is not about becoming an obstreperous and difficult person, but just observing the strength appearing within you as you become clearer about what is true for you. If you value yourself sufficiently and are true to yourself, it will be easier to make decisions that support you better.

As you become truer to yourself, others will honour and respect you more, and will be less likely to stand in your way. The idea here is not to make life difficult for others, but to find ways of honouring them and their needs, that will also honour you. These are 'win win' situations.

For example:

I don't have to attend every Rotary Club meeting.
　　And if I want to attend one meeting every three months, I can.
I don't have to read all the professional journals that come into the office.
　　And if I want to read some of them, I can.
I don't have to prove to my mother that I love her by doing everything she asks.
　　And if I want to show her how much I love her, I can buy her some flowers and tell her directly.

Actively promote your health, wealth and happiness and you will be enhancing your inner strength. Consider for a moment what wealth means for you. We are constantly bombarded by what represents 'wealth' via advertising, and those who are promoting how we spend money such as on the fast car, brand new house, exotic holidays, and so forth. There is a link between the symbol that represents financial wealth and the experience of well-being that has a deeper motivation for us. If you were to examine some of those external symbols, you might discover more about the experiences in life that are important to you.

There may be many other, and possibly less expensive ways, that you can generate certain experiences in your life as alternatives to the car, house or holiday.

For example, supposing you wanted to buy a larger home with more facilities, such as an extra bedroom, a room for the children, larger garden or swimming pool. If you had that larger house, how would you be feeling differently? How would the quality of your life be improved? One possibility here is that you get a sense of there being more upkeep involved, and you decide that a larger house is something you do not want.

However, say the qualities you would enjoy more of included, for example, relaxation, peace, freedom. Now ask yourself how you could have more of these qualities, in other ways. What could you be doing differently in your life *now* to promote more relaxation, peace and freedom? It might be having a weekend break; or spending fewer evenings working late; or it might be cutting back on some activities that do not support you fully, and which put you under stress.

Put your wealth, or well-being, back into your own hands and out of the direction of advertisers, peer pressure and other external forces. The exercise of that self-discipline will place you in a stronger position for achieving the goal of a larger home, if in fact that is something you really want. In any event, you will have already built within you the qualities you want, and those qualities will not be dependent upon an 'outer' object, symbol or result.

Creating your inner strength has to do with self-discipline and exercising your *choice muscle*. This is your ability to relax, let go of the limitation and switch into a positive focus. Each moment, you have the option to choose how you direct your thinking. You can also monitor closely what you set up, or agree to do.

There is a very subtle aspect to the Action/Productivity Cycle from *Clear Away Blocks* which is important for gaining inner strength and clarity. You may recall from that chapter that every time you enter into any agreement with yourself, or anyone else, some of your unconscious energy begins to get to work on bringing about the outcome you have agreed. This is fine and good if you follow through actively on what you have agreed. If you do not, you undermine yourself with a degree of confusion, rather like driving a car in forward and reverse at the same time.

We may be saying things without fully intending to follow through, such as:

Tomorrow, I shall get up at 6 a.m. and run for 5 miles
I am cutting ice cream out of my diet
I will read Barbara's script
I will clean the car at the weekend

Inside of you, there is a confusion, like having too many irons in the fire, and one result can be fatigue, not from having done too much, but simply from having taken more commitments upon yourself than you can reasonably fulfil. Not only do you suffer, but you risk losing the respect and love of other people as you let them down.

One of the most challenging and difficult responses we have to give to other people sometimes is the answer 'no' to a request. As a good friend, you may have a sense of obligation to do something which goes against your grain; or you may fear losing them as friends because you are not willing to comply with their request.

However, for the purpose of building your strength:

- Monitor what you agree to do
- Be careful to take on only what you are willing to fulfil and complete
- Make fewer commitments if necessary

- Re-negotiate with the person(s) concerned (including yourself) if you no longer wish to follow through with the agreement.

Exercising the strength to eliminate unnecessary distractions is like clearing the weeds from your path to fulfilment. Your clarity will increase as you become leaner and fitter in your commitments.

As you aim to strengthen yourself, notice that you may be challenged with opportunities to flex the choice muscle. The process is exhilarating as you come more and more into alignment with what you want, and manufacture less of the blocks and deadwood that would inhibit you.

Your creativity and imagination can come into play in different, unfamiliar situations and so that you can exercise your positive responses to them. Or you may enjoy challenging yourself in familiar situations with different ways of accomplishing the same, even small, things, such as your routine for getting up in the morning, or your drive to work. What can you do to further enrich your inner worlds?

For example, supposing you took up a new, physically challenging sport or adventure, such as river rafting, abseiling or parachuting, you might discover new strengths and capabilities. Or you could take up a new hobby and get to know how to relate with a different set of people.

The point here is that if everything around you stays relatively static and unchanging, like living 'on automatic', you do not give yourself the variety of experience that will make living fully rewarding. As you develop your ability to choose clearly for yourself in many circumstances, you will gain the greater direction over your unconscious resources of vitality and wisdom.

What is wisdom? Practice, practice, practice.

The person who has taken risks in his/her life has gained a wealth of experience and wisdom about the way life works. So dare yourself to do new things, and dare to do familiar things differently. Practise exercising your power and freedom to choose in each situation the most positive, rewarding outcome, both inwardly and outwardly.

Enhancing your inner strength does not mean that you bulldoze your way through your frailties, nor does it mean building a wall around your sensitivities. Inner strength is not a force that you use to fight others.

Even if in your physical makeup you enjoy excellent health and the full use of all your faculties, it is likely that in certain situations, you will feel mentally and emotionally challenged, even 'inadequate', or to put it more darkly, 'handicapped'. It just seems as though you are not equipped to deal with certain circumstances.

You might find it helpful, in those dark moments when you can find no obvious, clear positive way through, to reflect that sometimes 'the darkest hour is just before dawn'. You are not alone. There are others who have probably had similar moments. It does take strength, and considerable courage, at these times to admit to your frailty and seek assistance.

Even within the most ebullient and outwardly successful people, you may notice a softness and vulnerability, not necessarily strongly on display, but nevertheless it is there. Your sensitivity or vulnerability is, paradoxically perhaps, a door to your inner strength. Batten it down, or wall it up, and you lose the value of your sensitivity.

The same lowering of your defences which would enable you to be 'wounded' allows for an openness through which you may also be 'blessed'. In becoming truer to yourself, you will gain if you can honour and respond to that vulnerability. The open door allows a passage for perceiving the world more accurately and clearly. It also permits clearer communication from you to the outer world, not necessarily verbally, but also in many other dimensions, such as in your body language and facial expressions.

Your vulnerability is an important aspect of your inner strength. Through your vulnerability you gain the power to receive the resources you need, both from within yourself and from the world around you. Look at the example of a small child who is not equipped with the full range of skills for managing himself in the world. His vocabulary is limited and he views life with a certain innocence, openness and trust. He perhaps sees the world around him in a fresh way, just as it is, without the colour of adult emotions. In the best of circumstances, most adults are drawn to protect and care for such a child.

Ideally, in our maturity, we can still retain a childlike view in which we are open to see life very clearly as it is, beyond the mechanisms we generally use to function effectively. When we wish, we can tap into the child within us and once again, be vulnerable to and make contact with a pure source of inner knowledge.

In this next exercise, allow your vulnerability to be represented by a young child, seeing the world with openness and innocence. You might like to give the child a name. If your name is Alice, you could call the child Little Alice.

Walking With Strength

Take some time to be completely alone with yourself, undisturbed for 15 to 30 minutes. You might like to play some soft music in the background. This is an experiment in which you will be bringing your creative imagination into play in a dialogue form in which the 'adult you' talks with the 'child you'.

You will need to set aside any feelings of awkwardness or embarrassment and be patient at first as you establish contact with this inner child. If in the past your approach to life has been somewhat 'macho' (women can also be macho) the child may take a while to gain the confidence to step forward and respond to you. Primarily your task is to be a good listener and allow the child maximum freedom to say what is on his/her mind. Love and encourage the child to express his/her concerns and interests.

Take a pad of notepaper and start with your initial on

the left side of the sheet. Open the conversation and put an initial for the child, listen for a response and write that down. You might choose a topic that has to do with one of your objectives and ask for 'your' child's thoughts or feelings about that objective, or the way you are going about it. Or you could choose a situation to discuss about which you have had some mixed feelings. Keep any questions open and uncritical.

Your page could look something like this:

A Hello, how are you feeling today?

LA Quite good. I didn't like being with Carol yesterday.

A Why was that?

LA I don't know really. I did not feel comfortable with her.

A Was she critical or unkind to you in some way?

LA Not exactly that.

A Can you say a bit more about your feelings, about what happened?

LA I felt she was pushy and demanding and wanted me to do things her way and I didn't want to.

A Is there anything else?

LA Do we have to see her again tomorrow?

A Not necessarily. If we do, how can I make it easier for you?

LA Don't spend more time with her than we absolutely have to.

A I'll see what I can do. Let's see also how we can make the short time we do spend with her more fun. Then we can have a treat afterwards – what would you like?
etc.

With practice and patience, you will discover a valuable resource in your inner child that will assist you to make the most of your feelings and responses. It is important that in relating with your child you demonstrate caring, courtesy and consideration. However, you as the adult have the final say and choice in determining your direction and actions. Your choices are made after consultation with, and then with the co-operation of, the child.

This exercise may assist you in resolving inner conflicts if they arise and give you a clear step forward. The child within you has a right to feel disturbed and uncomfortable while you are making changes in your life. The adult 'you' can give reassurance and encouragement by staying in touch and maintaining a dialogue of support, much as you might do in a family situation. It is a way in which you can bring yourself more fully into alignment with your new vision and in this way, strengthen your inner resolve.

Creating a safe environment for an open inner dialogue is a part of having a safe harbour in which to rest and recharge yourself for your passages ahead. Learning to listen uncritically to yourself is worth practising.

Becoming more vulnerable as a person does not mean wearing your heart on your sleeve and being a victim of the 'slings and arrows of outrageous fortune'. It is more an inner frame of reference in which you monitor closely all kinds of input as it comes to you, and select and direct consciously the thoughts, words and actions that will enhance your positive purpose. This vulnerability assists you to stay in tune with this positive purpose beyond the challenges and obstacles that would shake you off it.

Value your vulnerability as an asset. One barrier that you may have set up to protect your vulnerability might be that of not valuing yourself. In some way you do not live up to a high standard, or expectation, of yourself. So rather than let the rest of the world see your imperfections, you hide them. In hiding, you lose sight not only of the weaknesses but also the strengths.

Success is sometimes equated with a perfect state towards which you can aim, but in fact, would never achieve. So that, in a perfect world, with ideal conditions, you would be the perfect father/husband/son; mother/wife/daughter; millionaire, head-of-corporate-empire, president/chairman; 100 per cent loving and giving, peaceful and harmonious, generous and loyal, 100 per cent of the time, in fact, the all-round success, that everyone recognizes as such. Striving for, but failing to achieve, such perfection produces within us a feeling of guilt.

That pattern of guilt is insidious and consumes personal strength. You may have done nothing worse than having simply failed to live up to impossible expectations that you imposed on yourself. Then you live with the stress of striving to prove to yourself and others that you are not so bad after all, when you were not really 'bad' in the first place. What a fatiguing waste of effort. This attitude of 'I'm not good enough' may not even be your own direct creation. You may have 'inherited' it from a parent, who similarly had done nothing radically 'wrong'.

The sins of the parents get passed on. Thus, the burden of guilt can be deeply hidden. What is more, your behaviour can reinforce this sense of guilt by being rebellious, or 'anti-social', however you have defined 'social' or acceptable. All of this would really go to prove that you are unacceptable. And so on.

By using the technique of dialoguing with your inner child, you may uncover some of the hidden burdens that take away from your experience of a successful lifestyle. As a loving 'parent' to yourself, you can restore the loving appreciation for who you are, and heal the hurts of a critical attitude towards yourself.

Have you ever heard yourself say anything like the following: 'I am not a good enough person to have/be/do what I really want. I do not deserve to have all the money, fulfilment, marriage, freedom, love, because I am not good enough'? A similar limiting belief may be concealed by statements like: 'What I have now is good enough for me', implying that you would like better but perhaps do not deserve to have it. Or: 'My life is absolutely fine the way it is', which, if not really true, is possibly denying that in your heart of hearts you would like to effect some positive changes. Such beliefs act as a burden of self-rejection. Unconsciously, you behave so as to fulfil these underlying beliefs in yourself.

Spending time looking beyond patterns of self-rejection, if you have any, will take you a step nearer enhancing your inner strength. It is useful to know that you may be carrying an inaccurate image of yourself as being in some way not worthy of whatever form of success you seek. As you discover and re-focus on your qualities, you will find it easier to relax and receive the best that life has to offer you.

The remedy for self-rejection is to rebuild the sense of your intrinsic value. Do not attempt to analyse your past shortcomings by dwelling on them, but choose instead to re-align yourself with the qualities you want to be enjoying more of; choose to relax into your future vision now. Switch from the contracted experiences of the past into the fullness you now want.

You may have experienced envy towards someone because they had the very thing you wanted, but so far have failed to achieve for yourself. The emotion is depleting, but may serve to inform you more clearly what you want for yourself. Now that you are more in touch with your motivation, you can constructively channel your energies out of the knot of resentment towards achieving your goal.

The next exercise will assist you to get in touch with you as the winner in your life. The exciting aspect of creating the winner inside you is that you will put yourself in a good position for assisting others to become winners in their own eyes. When you do have what you want, you may feel freer to assist others to gain what they want.

Your Winning Experience

Earlier you were bringing to mind your 'wins' for a period of time in your life. Now, cast your mind over your whole life and allow one win to pop forward. It could be relatively small and still work well in this exercise.

This is an exercise which you might like to put on audio cassette. Take time and a place in which you will be undisturbed and take the phone off the hook. You could look upon this time as being in your safe harbour, a time for recharging and renewing yourself. Make sure you are comfortable and relaxed.

Close your eyes and begin to tune inwardly. Take a deep breath . . . let that breath go and become more relaxed . . . take in another deep breath . . . and as you let that breath go, imagine the air very clear and light all around you . . . like being on the top of a mountain, with a clear blue sky for as far as you can see . . . there is a pure whiteness of snow on the mountaintops . . . an exhilaration in the freshness of the air as you breathe it into you . . . Begin to feel within yourself . . . the magnificence . . . the great height . . . the splendour . . . majesty . . . timelessness at the peak of the mountain . . .

At this peak . . . right now . . . bring to mind your winning experience . . . What was it you achieved? . . . Notice all the details of your win . . . Who else was with you? . . . Where were you? . . . What were you wearing? . . . what colours . . . what fabrics . . . textures? . . . Are there any special smells associated with your win? . . . Any flavours? . . . What can you hear? . . . Applause? . . . Appreciation? . . . Your own acknowledgement? . . . What were the rewards that came with this win? . . .

What qualities . . . or feelings do you enjoy with your win? . . . How do you feel at your best? . . . Notice these qualities . . . and breathe deeply into them . . . so that they expand . . . Let those qualities vibrate within you . . . Become so totally alive with the winning qualities that you are radiant . . . Not only are you filled with the richness of this winning experience . . . but the world around you glistens . . . sparkles . . . and shines with the wealth of who you are . . .

Now . . . very gently and in your own timing . . . become more aware of the room you are in . . . open your eyes . . . maintaining the contact with your winning qualities.

> *Take a notebook and make a note of those winning qualities, words and phrases that describe you at the peak of your success.*

As you take steps to expand into your vision of success, your confidence will similarly expand to promote the arrival of your success. Your safe harbour will be a place in which you can nurture your deepest inner fulfilment. Explore and discover for yourself ways in which you can revitalize yourself on a regular basis, a programme which you can reasonably incorporate into your life.

Your immediate cry might be that your life is already so full, you hardly have enough time to accomplish all you need to do as it is. Nurturing all this inner stuff is all very well, but I have other things far too pressing. There are not enough hours in the day . . .

Wait a minute. Are you one of those people who will always be 'too busy' to ever enjoy the rewards of your success? Even when you have considerable financial wealth, will you still be driven in pursuit of gaining more and more in the outer world? Will the drama and excitement of the fast lane block you from some of life's finer pleasures?

In the western world, it is not somehow natural to meditate daily and yet many of us feel that need. The next exercise is a version of a process called Autogenic Training, which enables you to switch off from the world by issuing commands to your body to relax. It does not take very long to do for the benefits to be experienced: five minutes, three times a day.

Autogenic Training

While you are learning this technique, it will be useful to be in a quiet place. Once you are familiar with it, you may be able to do it sitting in a train, standing in a queue or at other times when your mind might otherwise be preoccupied.

The two best positions for your body are either lying flat, with your legs straight out and your hands by your side, or sitting comfortably in a chair with your spine supporting you properly, your arms and legs uncrossed, feet flat on the floor.

With your eyes closed, you will be repeating commands to your body and experiencing your body's response. The commands are as follows, with abbreviated initials that you might like to write on a sheet of paper as a reminder.

RAH My right arm is heavy

ALHW My arms and legs are heavy and warm

SPR My solar plexus is radiant

NSH My neck and shoulders are heavy

FCC My forehead is cool and clear

BBM My body breathes me

IAAP I am at peace

Repeat each command three times and experience the response of your body.

It is best at first to train yourself by repeating all the commands several times, so that you become familiar with the experience of them. Then the process becomes automatic. As you focus on your body relaxing, you will gradually, if temporarily, let go of the concerns of your mind and emotions.

Then spend five minutes in a relaxed state before getting up; take five minutes in the middle of the day, where you will be uninterrupted; the final five minutes last thing at night before sleeping. These mini-holidays throughout your day will strengthen and refresh you. It is one of the most effective ways of giving yourself a short break.

We often store tension in our neck and shoulders. You may notice yourself, or others, with shoulders tightened up around the ears. When we relax, our shoulders drop and our breathing is improved. Shortness in our breath, or shallow breathing, inhibits a relaxed frame of mind.

If you are experiencing tightness around the neck and shoulders, you may find it beneficial to repeat inwardly:

My neck and shoulders are heavy

and allow your shoulders to drop. You can even do this with other people around you in a challenging situation.

This next technique you can use to heal and repair any inadequacy in your self-image. Rather than dwell on the shortcomings, you can switch into the more accurate inner perception of your qualities. As you enhance your view of yourself, and relax into feeling good about yourself, you will be more open and receptive to making your life easier.

Up until now, it is likely that in your makeup you have patterns of denial relative to your new picture of success. To step forward into your expanded vision, you will need to grow beyond the previous image you have held of yourself. The inner step will be one of affirming the new qualities within you which will sustain your growth and be a part of that new picture.

First of all, it is important to accept that the beliefs of a lifetime are probably deeply rooted within you. However, deeper still are the positive qualities that so far have lain dormant until such time as you are ready to claim them. If in any of the guided visualization exercises so far you have experienced qualities that are not yet part of your everyday experience, these are the ones that are ready to be given fuller emphasis in your life. This could be both inwardly and outwardly.

Earlier, in *Unlock Your Attitude,* the use of language was shown as a way of maintaining a positive, forward-moving direction in your life. There is a simple technique, Affirmation, which strengthens an improved self-image and beliefs about yourself. As with most of the exercises, experiment with this one in small steps if it is a new process for you. With Affirmations, you can transform your inner blocks into outer performance through changing your attitude and beliefs. So, for example, rather than feel inadequate in certain circumstances, you can begin to envisage yourself effectively demonstrating your skill, talent and capability.

The only time in which we have any real flexibility and command over our inner environment is in the moment right now. We cannot change the feelings we had in the past, even two minutes ago. They were what they were. We have no control fully in the present moment over the feelings we will have in the future, although we can be guiding ourselves towards our preferences. But it is in this moment now that we can choose where we focus. The affirmation we make now strengthens us in maintaining that direction. The images, pictures and experiences that we make up, or create vividly, become part of our internal reality. That internal reality is instrumental in bringing about the outer results.

Is anger an emotion that you would like to replace with increased peacefulness? The images and words that you might like to be introducing into yourself would be those of harmony, objectivity and calm, for example. Do you want to have more fun and enjoyment? Would you like to be more relaxed about your financial affairs? Would more enthusiasm or vitality make life easier for you?

Affirming is simple and powerful. You will find, when you introduce a new thought into your unconscious, that the results come to you in ways that you might never have been able to imagine or work out with your conscious mind.

Guidelines for Making Affirmations

1. Each affirmation is stated positively, with no negatives so that each word of the affirmation has a positive

image for you.

For example:

'I never get angry when I am caught in traffic.'
Although there is a positive idea here, it is stated
negatively. It is better stated:

'I am calm and relaxed, making the best use of
my time, even when I am in slow-moving traffic.'

2. It must be stated clearly, and be something that you
can imagine for yourself and that you really want.

For example:

'I expect to be strong when I meet my boss
tomorrow.'

This would look better as:

'I am clear and confident of achieving my
winning objectives with my boss.'

3. To be most effective, an affirmation is stated in the first
person, present tense. First person because the only
person over whom you have any real control or
direction is yourself. Present tense because you are
introducing the new thought pattern right now, and
again, the only time over which you have any control
or direction is now.

For example:

'My secretary will produce this letter perfectly.'
As much as you would like, you really cannot
determine your secretary's attitudes and
performance in the future.

'I am clearly communicating my needs and
instructions, enthusiastically supporting my
highly skilled secretary in her success.'

4. Use words that stimulate and inspire you into the
strengths and qualities you want to have more fully in
your life. Let your imagination go free here – an
affirmation is only for you.

For example:

'I am determined.'

An affirmation simply stated can be powerful and effective. However, you could experiment with expanding the statement with more colour and flair so that your inner attention is called fully into play.

'With ease, confidence and enthusiasm, I am persistent and purposeful, valuing myself as I courageously address each step towards my success.'

5. Choose affirmations that match your priorities. Make sure that they are in line with your overall picture. Take care to limit the number you use at any one time. Like any other agreement you undertake, make sure that it is one which you will want to follow through and complete.

These outlines are a basis for the technique. Feel free to explore and discover how they can most effectively work for you.

Here are some examples that will illustrate the process. You might like to adopt, or adapt, them for your own use. As a beginning, choose no more than three to work with at a time, say over a week or two, so that you can discover how the process works, and observe the changes taking place within you.

- I am strong, courageous and powerful
- I am abundantly healthy, wealthy and happy
- I enjoy being me
- I am clear, decisive and wise in my thoughts, words and actions
- When I wake up in the morning, I am relaxed and happy
- It's easy for me to be true to my heartfelt purpose and mission in life

- I accept, love and appreciate myself
- I take care to maintain a healthy balance in my life
- I am loving my full and enriching friendships
- I am an excellent listener
- I treasure my vulnerability and sensitivity
- I am having more fun enjoying the benefits of my successful lifestyle
- I am an action person, very effective and efficient in challenging situations
- I express myself clearly, with humour and trust
- I am true to myself and communicate with honesty and love
- I am serene and peaceful in achieving my successes
- It is fun for me to make my life easy
- I enjoy being enthusiastic and effective
- I love and respect myself, just as I am
- I have a good memory and I easily remember anything that is important to me
- I have great stamina and energy and I am enjoying life to the full
- My mind is positively focused, filling my life with harmony, balance and well-being
- I look at the world in a positive light and envisage the best possible outcomes in everything I do
- I am creating the best for myself, attracting the best in others and delight in finding the best in the world
- I take on only that which I can fulfil with ease and grace
- I am grateful for my unique combination of skills, talents and abilities
- I have pleasure in using to the full my gifts and qualities
- I enjoy my enthusiasm and vitality
- When life is challenging for me, I bring forward my greatest strengths
- I transform my blocks into blessings
- I am treating all problems as opportunities to grow in wisdom and love

The following questions may further assist you in choosing your affirmations:
1. What **positive words** will help to motivate you beyond your blocks?
2. What would you need to tell yourself to **overcome** your limiting beliefs?
3. What **personal qualities** do you have that contribute to your self-confidence?
4. What **strengths** would you like to have more of and reinforce?
5. What new **habits** would improve the quality of your life?

Once you have chosen your first three affirmations, write them, one each, on record or index cards. Keep them in a wallet and refer to them during the day when you have time on your hands and might want to give yourself a 'boost'. The best time for introducing and anchoring new attitudes and beliefs into your unconscious, when you are most receptive, is either last thing at night or first thing in the morning, before you are fully engaged in the day's events. You could also write them on sticky labels and keep them in a diary.

Do not disclose your affirmations to anyone apart from yourself. This would be like wearing your heart on your sleeve. Other people, even unwittingly, can easily discourage you and drive you back into a former pattern of limitation, failure and sense of lack.

As you read each affirmation, imagine, as vividly as you can, that desired experience as if it were happening right now. Relax into it and enjoy it. You can even breathe in deeply, and imagine filling yourself with the new qualities as you do so. Be creative and have fun with this process. In fact, you may find that the more you bring your imagination into play here, the better your results.

Affirmations work with repetition. Do not expect any results if you just read them through once. Repeat them while waiting in traffic. Sing them operatically if you are alone. Or, if you are running, or swimming or walking, you can be turning them over in your mind. If you are on your own, and outside of hearing distance, stand up, stretch and say them dramatically out loud with full, dramatic emphasis in your voice. Pretend that you are in a football stadium, addressing a crowd of thousands. Be careful to take in a deep breath as you do so, and do not strain your voice.

If you are more visually inclined, you can have your affirmations illustrated, or written in beautiful lettering that will make a strong impression on your mind. Put them in a diary that you see often. The more vivid the picture, the greater the impact. Keep experimenting until you discover the best possible form for you.

If words are powerful in bringing about transformation in your thinking and outlook, images themselves are possibly even more direct a form of communication with your inner self. The next exercise is one in which you can illustrate your new desired experiences, where the images you choose represent the qualities you are affirming.

A Treasure Map of Your Inner Strengths

For this exercise, you will need magazines, scissors, glue and a sheet of card or strong paper. You might like to have a note of the qualities you are strengthening within you as a reminder.

Go through the magazines and cut out the images that most reflect to you the qualities and inner strengths you want to affirm. The association between the image and the quality may not be obvious to anyone but you. For example, an open window might reflect openness to you; an apple, good health; clouds, freedom; a diamond, clarity; a clown, cheerfulness; shoes, stability.

Once again, it is probably better that no one else does know what the images mean for you. Arrange and stick the pictures on to your card in a collage. However it comes out is fine, so long as it is vivid and has appeal for you. You might like to buy a simple frame for the Treasure Map and have it on a wall, or standing on a desk or table.

Just seeing it around you, even in the periphery of your vision, will make its influence felt because it will act as a constant reminder of your strengthened self-image, and gradually replace the former lesser self-image in your unconscious.

Until you are fully demonstrating your new qualities and strengths, you can experiment in your imagination having them. Imagine yourself in a variety of situations and events where a negative quality that has sabotaged you in the past is now replaced by the perfect strength that enables you to feel and behave differently.

It is possible to transform a negative experience that we have held within ourselves into a more preferable outcome so that rather than hang on to the pain of the past, we can fully believe that something else really happened. This is a means of healing long-term hurts in relationships, most especially that of the relationship with yourself. Healing and forgiving the hurts will awaken you to more of your strengths.

The course of your daily life itself may provide you with times to test out your new strengths as they are growing within you. These 'tests', when they occur, will give you a measure of that strength. If you feel you have 'failed', or weakened, it may be more accurate to note that you have more attention to give before that strength is fully in place, supporting you. Tests may highlight where you have more 'work' yet to do.

Allow time for the positive effects to materialize fully. Some qualities that you are affirming may be so deeply buried that they take a year or two before they are actively a part of you. For example, if you have been rigid and formal in your attitude, you might want to affirm more spontaneity and fun. Choose situations in which you can exercise these new qualities, and be forgiving towards yourself if you feel yourself slipping back into old patterns.

You are building inner strength to give yourself the confidence to attract and enjoy success. While it is primarily for you, it will also enhance the lives of those around you. Your inner strength will serve others, and will be further reinforced in this way. As you interact with others with greater inner mastery, you will be able to appreciate your progress because they will reflect it back to you.

One meaning of the word 'create' is: 'to grow, or cause to grow'. The fact is that you already have considerable inner strength as a living being. Then, what is the source of your inner strength, and how might you 'cause it to grow'?

Take a deep breath for a moment and hold it until you are aware of your heartbeat. As long as you live, you breathe, for the most part unconsciously, and your heart does its work without reward. Given all the obstacles there are to life continuing, such as cars, planes and other transport, disease in many forms, wars and terrorists, it is a miracle that there are so many people sustaining life on the world.

Perhaps the heart, sustaining life the way it does, is one of the greatest symbols of strength. What are the qualities, associated with the heart, that you might wish to grow? Below are some of them. You may wish to add more.

Qualities of the Heart

- courage
- willingness
- caring
- integrity
- compassion
- sincerity
- clarity
- generosity
- loyalty
- enthusiasm

- commitment
- kindness
- intuition
- love
- inspiration
- warmth
- wisdom
- trust
- giving
- freedom
- grace

- devotion
- encouragement
- sensitivity
- humour
- peace
- openness
- truth
- spontaneity
- receiving
- joy
- gratitude

Amplifying the qualities associated with your heart, the essence of who you are, will strengthen you in your life's purpose. Heroic figures in literature and history demonstrate many of these qualities and inspire us, as do contemporary sports figures, mountaineers and round-the-world yachters, or leaders that demonstrate compassion and wisdom in relating with other people. They are known and noted for overcoming visible hazards. What has given them their winning attitudes?

For this next exercise, bring a personality to mind, someone that you admire and who inspires you. They may be living, dead or fictional; male or female. The person you have chosen will be one who demonstrates the qualities of the heart, those qualities that will assist you in furthering your own aims. Imagine that the qualities already exist within you, and that you can now amplify them.

Building Your Winning Attitude

You may like to close your eyes here to get in touch with your imagination. Bring your 'hero' to mind, notice how he/she stands and moves, and possibly how he/she is dressed. Look at his/her face – what do you notice about it? Listen to him/her talk – how does his/her voice sound to you? Imagine him/her now in a situation which is challenging. How does he/she respond and react to it? What qualities do you notice him/her demonstrating? How is he/she winning?

What is special about his/her manner?

Make some notes about the qualities you observed in your hero. Now write for yourself a short description of you, demonstrating these same qualities in an imagined situation. This could be a challenge that you are currently facing, like a meeting with the bank manager, confronting an issue with a child, giving a presentation at a sales conference or running a marathon. As each challenging moment comes to mind, bring forward a winning quality so that your outcome is that of a winner. Be a hero to yourself.

A winning key here is to envisage any other party, with whom you interact, also gaining so that you can walk away freely from the exchange.

The greatest barriers and frontiers you will ever have to overcome are within you. Other people and circumstances will merely reflect to you the nature of your obstacles. The heart, as we know it symbolically, represents the common ground, the link that exists between people of all ages, nationalities, sexes and cultures. Demonstrate the qualities of the heart and you transcend the barriers that exist within and around you. Experience and gradually grow into these qualities and you will find yourself effectively in the driver's seat of your life.

One of the most precious gifts you have, and have possibly not fully developed yet, is that of your intuition or deep inner knowing and guidance. There is a wisdom within and constantly available to you, once you learn how to listen, respond and work with it. This wisdom is sometimes referred to as the 'still small voice'. With practice you may discover how to discern when you are being given valuable information that can direct you towards your success. This is a process of inner attunement.

The first part of creating inner strength has to do with

learning the discipline of loving towards yourself. This is the
process that builds strength and resolve. An additional benefit
is one of attuning yourself to your latent resources of wisdom,
clarity and intuitive understanding.

The next exercise is a guided visualization in which your
inner guidance will be represented by an enlightened being,
a wise person or spiritual master. Again, this person could be
living, dead or fictional so long as you can bring him/her
vividly into your imagination. This is an exercise which may
work better if pre-recorded so that you can concentrate
inwardly without any distractions around you.

Tuning Into The Inner Master

*Make sure you are comfortable and undisturbed, phone off the
hook, door closed. Begin by taking in a deep breath and relaxing
. . . Let go of that breath . . . Breathe deeply again . . . and
let every muscle in your body relax . . . Notice any thoughts
going through your mind . . . like clouds passing across a blue
summer sky . . . Let them pass . . . Observe your feelings . . .
and let them go too . . . You are much more than your feelings,
anxieties and concerns . . . Allow yourself to become very
peaceful, empty and still inside . . .*

*Bring any quality of the heart to mind . . . and notice where
you are with it . . . a place in nature – a mountain . . . or
forest . . . meadow . . . lake . . . beach . . . a garden . . .
Notice your quality of the heart in every aspect of the world
around you . . . Breathe it into you deeply and become at one
with it . . .*

*Now invite into this scene your master force . . . welcome
them to it . . . You might like to embrace this being . . . or take
them by the hand and feel the reassurance they offer to you . . .
If there is anything you would like to ask them . . . about your
vision or dreams . . . any situation that you are currently
facing . . . ask, and listen for their reply . . . take as much time
as you need with your friend . . .*

When you have asked all you want . . . your master turns to you with a gift . . . and you receive it with delight . . . what is the gift? . . . what does this gift mean for you? . . . what does it represent? . . . Thank your friend and let them go . . . fading from the scene . . . so that you are now once again on your own . . . and filled with a greater sense of who you truly are . . .

Breathe deeply and amplify the fullness of who you are . . . And now very gradually . . . in your own timing . . . become once more aware of your room . . . and your surroundings . . . maintaining contact within you of your greater presence . . .

Take a notebook or journal and write any observations you would like about your experience, the guidance and wisdom you received, the qualities of your gift.

With an open mind, you might like to explore how you can incorporate this guidance into your life. A caution here is to select carefully how you use the guidance you receive. Be wise in your conscious choices. It is important that you both:

learn to listen carefully to your inner knowledge
and
learn how best to utilize this information in your life.

There are times when we lose belief in ourselves, and to gain re-direction from the heart, the centre of our lives, enables us to progress. As the strengths are already within you, you have firstly to awaken yourself to those strengths. Then 'cause them to grow' by keeping them in your sight. You will find that what you focus on will become more available to you and more a part of your successful lifestyle.

Chapter 5
Expect Success

It may surprise you to know that you were born with an inbuilt mechanism for success. For the mechanism to work effectively, you need to have a very clear impression within yourself of the success you want, the goals and objectives you are aiming for. In *Create Inner Strength*, the emphasis was on recognizing and enhancing your innate qualities. With a stronger self-image, you can direct yourself towards improving the quality of your external lifestyle.

In *Set Personal Objectives*, Sections 2 and 3 for your goals were outlined as follows:

Section 2:
    Relationships with Family/Home
    Relationships with Friends/Colleagues
    Service
    Personal Hobby/Recreation Pursuit and
Section 3
    Career/Status
    Salary/Income
    Investments
    House/Car/Holidays

Section 2 largely concerns the relationship with yourself and others and Section 3, broadly speaking, your relationship with the more material aspects of the world.

There is a skill in choosing the outer targets and goals which you can reasonably attain, and yet which still have a sufficient element of challenge or stimulation to provide inner satisfaction on completion. Like any skill, selecting the most appropriate objectives for yourself may take practice, may take making some mistakes in the process of discovering what is most meaningful for you.

In *Set Personal Objectives*, there was an exercise to explore the meaning 'success' has for you. Initially, you could begin to form a picture of your life three years ahead from now. Such a picture might necessarily lack detail. Many factors can come into play within a three-year period which are impossible to anticipate. However, you may begin by determining the qualities you wish to be enjoying more of in life.

The following exercise may assist you in further clarifying not just a single success for yourself, such as climbing a mountain or achieving a set time in a marathon, but what would constitute a successful lifestyle, in the areas of fulfilling relationships with other people and your material resources.

In *Create Inner Strength*, there was an exercise which involved making a Treasure Map, a collage, of your inner strengths and qualities, where the images you selected represented qualities. So a photograph of clear water might represent clarity for you; a pine forest, serenity; a beach, enjoyment.

This time, the Map may include not only images which represent qualities, but also pictures of the specific kind of house, or car, or relationship you want, whatever makes up your picture of a successful lifestyle. You may need to collect a number of illustrated magazines and gradually gather together your pictures.

A Treasure Map of Your Successful Lifestyle

Allow yourself plenty of time and opportunity to look around you and gather the pictures that most represent the lifestyle you would like to enjoy.

If you are not married or in a long-term relationship, and would like to have a fulfilling partnership with a spouse, look for images that most closely represent the qualities you want to enjoy more of with someone you love. How might you be spending your time with this other person? Where would you be? What would you be doing together? Are there any images connected with a marriage/relationship?

What sort of home would you like to live in? How might that be furnished? Would you like a garden, an orchard, flowers, vegetables? Is there a hobby or sport you would like to enjoy? A car you would like to own?

Is there a dream holiday that you would like to have? A tropical location, a safari, trekking in the Himalayas, visiting nature reserves or ancient historic sites, a world cruise?

What would contribute to your improved lifestyle now? What would be a greater picture of success as you might experience it? Are there any small, yet significant, changes that you could envisage?

Make your collage on whatever size of paper is most convenient and workable for you. It could be small enough to fit into a loose-leaf diary, or larger to frame and hang on a wall. Above all, make it vivid, enjoyable and appealing for you.

Having this collage visible within the periphery of your sight will contribute towards your inner expectation of success. The images will make an impression on you that will by-pass the doubts and negative attitudes of your mind and emotions.

This exercise has proved effective in attracting fulfilling relationships, a better career, holidays, desired bodyweight and even improved financial conditions. The images alone do not produce the results, of course, but as the impressions are made within us, we become drawn towards the actions and resources that bring about the reality we envision. When you are ready to make it, this Treasure Map will be a means of assisting you to focus your attention on your final destination in the process of adjustment in *Unlock Your Attitude*.

In progressing towards your successful lifestyle, you bring into play your inner success mechanism. This requires a certain watchfulness. The signs are all around you which tell you when you need to monitor what you are doing and make adjustments as necessary. For example, supposing you had had a stormy relationship with one of your parents and were now wanting to establish more loving communications. You would observe and monitor the times you lost your patience, or became angry, as being 'off course' towards your objective. You might need to stand back and work on healing and strengthening your own inner environment before expressing yourself outwardly towards your parents.

Your inner monitor will assist you to learn to recognize when you need to refine your approach, or make adjustments. The task is then one of experimenting to find the next effective course of action that will lead to the results you want.

Once you know where you are going, and you have prepared yourself to get there, this automatic monitor will prove a most valuable resource. As you head forward in the direction of your choice, it is like an adventure, embarking on a passage of discovery. You will find that every time you act, think or in some way lose sight of your aim, you will get a signal that will alert you and attract your attention in some way.

The 'signal' may show up in the form of an emotional, mental or physical block. It could be stress of some kind that produces symptoms such as a head cold, for example, which causes you to reflect on how you are going about your life. Emotions such as anger, irritation and depression can also cause you to re-evaluate your approach.

Your inner monitor works like an automatic pilot in aircraft, as mentioned earlier in *Set Personal Objectives*. The aircraft is set on course for a specific destination. Every time the plane travels 'off course', it is brought back in line with its target destination. The automatic pilot is very clear where it is going. All the instrumentation is set for arrival. However, between take off and landing, it is subject to wind currents and other atmospheric changes which are, at least partly, unpredictable. If you were to map the course of the aircraft, it would probably not be a straight line. More likely, it would be 'zig-zagged'.

The path towards our success similarly may not look like a straight line, once we have arrived and look back on it. One of the greatest challenges we may face on the way is not giving up in discouragement at those times we are apparently 'off course', having temporarily lost sight of our aims.

You may not value your inner monitor until you have had some experience observing how it functions. Once you have learned how it works and how to use it, your passage towards an improved quality of lifestyle becomes much more interesting and fun. The recognition of those times when you have gone 'off course' will always be within you. Other means by which you may be alerted can be within you as a feeling response, an intuition possibly, or by the people or events around you, which call your attention by seeming to obstruct you in some way.

For example, your world at times may seem to frustrate your every effort to get ahead. You may not be able to locate the physical tools or resources in order to take the next step. The loan you need may be out of your reach. The people with whom you work fail to deliver what they promise. Those you would like to love better seem to upset you more than ever. Or, you simply cannot put your finger on the next move you must make.

You may find yourself responding with fear, doubt, anger, depression. With practice, you can learn instead to stop, look and listen for the information being offered by the apparent block, rather than knock your head against a wall. Resistance to that information, or the denial of it, can even produce a headache or some other 'disease'.

When faced with such resistance, you could imagine that

your monitor is really friendly, calling your attention with a gift of some kind. Perhaps there is short cut you could use that would save you time and energy. Even though you thought you were on course, there may be an even more effective way towards what you want.

A line of questioning, like the following, may assist you to elicit and clarify your next steps and future direction. This process is similar to Sowing Seeds with Questions from *Set Personal Objectives*. Do not expect the answers to surface immediately, but be aware of information as it may come from many different sources, both within and around yourself.

Listening to Your Inner Monitor

Take a pen and pad of paper and ask as many questions as you can concerning the apparent halt in your progress. Then allow from 30 minutes to three days for information to surface. The questions below are examples. Add the ones that are most relevant for you.

- Is there a better way to accomplish what I want?
- Is my goal still in line with my overall purpose?
- Have I got caught in a needless distraction that will cost me unnecessary time or energy?
- Is there a more effective method available to me now?
- Who can assist me to get clearer?
- How can I stay more open and flexible?
- What information is available to me?
- How can I make better use of my time?
- How can I make the best use of my resources?
- What encouragement can I give to myself?

Like any obstacle that seemingly stops you in your tracks, you can strike out, punish or blame it, or the person representing it. You may even find yourself blaming or punishing yourself for having encountered the restraint. However, those approaches will not resolve the issue. A 'STOP' sign serves as a warning that you need to pay attention, look and listen before proceeding.

Those that we love and care for provide some of our times of greatest fulfilment. However, those to whom we are closest, and with whom we are at our most vulnerable, are also well placed to make us aware of our shortcomings when we are 'off course'. They are part of our immediate feedback system, offering STOP signs when we have gone out of line with ourselves.

Of course, some of the goals you set could involve primarily yourself, such as running in a marathon, climbing a mountain, or writing a novel. The main relationship you will be developing to reach those kinds of goals will be the one with yourself because your results start and end with you. Nevertheless, it is also likely that some of your goals will embrace others.

The most rewarding relationships are those in our closest, home environment, or those with whom our results depend in some way, such as colleagues, employees, employer.

A first step for you may be in redefining for yourself what your most successful relationships with others would be like. What might be your specific areas of improvement? Are there any ways in which you would like to be more confident? Would you like to experience a more honest and real contact with others where you can fully be yourself? How could you experience more loving and trust?

At home, or at school, you may have learnt and developed excellent strategies for competing against others to win attention and recognition. In games of competition, there are set rules for a set prize; there are winners and losers. Strategies for winning may involve fear, deceit and loneliness. Games of competition in the world have some value in challenging us to become resourceful, but only up to a point.

In competitive people environments, where there are winners and losers, we may put others down, see them as less than ourselves, in order to view ourselves as 'winners'. In a way, this is like taking three steps forward and one back. We waste our energy by misdirecting it. Similarly, we may have identified ourselves as 'losers' to some extent in life's game, so that we never allowed ourselves to win the 100 per cent that is potentially available to us. The more that we deny ourselves, the harder it becomes to welcome and embrace the winning of others. In fact, we may even resent them for it.

Freedom from this element of competition may be a key for you to open fully to your own expectation of success. Competition may produce inside you negative emotions that will limit you, such as a fear of losing because your self-esteem has been tied to your winning. Motivation out of fear is less rewarding than motivation out of loving.

Have you ever recognized a *fear of success* in yourself? That fear might be one of having to repeat yourself, or take on too much responsibility, become isolated, or lose something, or someone, you value. You may have become unwittingly subject to an internal rat race that you project in your view of the outside world.

One way of gaining your freedom from such inner conflicts is to love yourself and the negativity sufficiently to loosen its hold on you so that you can enjoy the full inner picture of your success. In this next exercise, you can transform limited expectations of success to gain the experience of freedom from them.

Your Freedom For Success

If you have ever experienced yourself being limited emotionally by any games of competition, you now have the opportunity to play a game of freedom. As much as you gain the freedom to pursue and receive success for yourself, you similarly allow others their own freedom, even if and when you do not 'approve' of their goals.

This exercise is a game of discovering for yourself the

images and symbols that represent freedom to you. This is not to say that your life will forever be free of conflict, but you may find you have increased the possibility to choose a freer expression when you want it.

For each of the following items from 1 to 20, make a note of the form that represents freedom to you. It does not have to be too serious. Do not be concerned if you do not get a form for every item. The examples given illustrate how this might look:

Examples

1.	An exercise	Swimming
2.	A piece of furniture	Oak table
3.	A country	Switzerland
4.	A city	London
5.	An island	Bermuda
6.	A colour	Green
7.	An animal	Bear
8.	An item of clothing	Tutu
9.	A building	Salisbury Cathedral
10.	A person	Jesus Christ
11.	A texture	Velvet
12.	A temperature	68 degrees
13.	A scene in nature	A beach
14.	An occupation	Public speaking
15.	A hobby	Gardening
16.	A sport	Sailing
17.	A holiday	Safari
18.	A fruit	Banana
19.	A vegetable	Carrot
20.	A sound	Ocean

From your own list of forms, select the ones that make the greatest impact on you, that most powerfully evoke the experience of freedom within you. With your eyes closed, become involved with each form so that you gain an increased feeling of freedom within you. If the symbol is active, such as a sport, envisage yourself doing it. Become the colour, the temperature, the texture, the sound. Relate with each form, however you can, with all your senses.

Into these feelings of freedom, now bring your full expectation of your successful lifestyle, the objectives and results you most want. From this vantage point, there is an ease and harmony, vitality and enthusiasm, within and around you.

This exercise to be most effective does perhaps take the willingness to love your life and all the advantages it potentially has for you. When negative emotions, generated by a competitive attitude, would seem to limit you, experiment by reaching into your experiences of freedom. The perspective of freedom will assist you in loving yourself through your limiting emotions and into your increased expectation of success.

You may be familiar with the idea of 'self-fulfilling prophecy'. If you believe a certain outcome will happen, you are getting closer to effecting that result. Similarly, in relation to people, your attitude or belief about how others will behave can influence their behaviour. Your expectation brings forward a matching set of results.

The exercise, Muscle Testing for Expansion, in *Unlock Your Attitude*, can be done with another person. Negative attitudes directed towards another person can weaken them in the same way that negative attitudes directed towards yourself weakens you. Conversely, holding a high positive regard for other people brings the best out of them by assisting them to be in touch with the best within them.

G B Shaw's play *Pygmalion* brought forward the principle of self-fulfilling prophecy in two ways. Firstly, Professor Henry Higgins 'transforms' an uncultured flower girl, Eliza Doolittle, into a sophisticated lady through his belief in his ability, and the expectation of influencing Eliza's behaviour. Secondly, and perhaps most importantly, Eliza herself dreamt of improving her station in life. Pinned up around the walls of her modest room were pictures of the sort of life she wanted to have, like a Treasure Map. Was it perhaps her own deep desire that drew to her the person who could assist her in effecting the changes she wanted?

Each of us is potentially a creator, with the power and ability to shape our own life. In addition, we also influence the lives of everyone around us. We can influence others by communicating either a positive or negative expectation towards them. We may not always be aware that we have both this power, and consequently, this choice.

Communication is subtle at times, especially with those who have a close association with us. They can somehow tune in to our innermost thoughts that we think we conceal. We communicate in many ways other than the spoken word. Our thoughts 'speak' for us. Our body language and facial expressions say much. The confidence we have in ourselves communicates confidence in others. Similarly, our own spirit of enthusiasm awakens others to their enthusiasm.

Project your encouragement, caring and appreciation and you will assist others to sparkle and shine. Contribute positively to others, or let them go and be free to pursue their lives in another arena where they can be successful.

In your relation with others, you can enjoy the freedom of being finally accountable for any responses you receive from them. What you communicate tends to be returned to you. As you sow, so you reap.

Establishing and maintaining good relations with people who have any investment in your life, personal or career, may result in the most rewarding aspect of your successful lifestyle. There is nothing so precious in the world as human life, your own, or that of anyone else.

Working successfully with people is the source from which extraordinary results, even apparent miracles, can come about. There is nothing so powerful as a team of two or more people co-operating with enthusiasm and single-mindedness on a set objective, each person honouring their personal motives and values, direction and purpose as they serve the group vision.

However you are moving towards a successful lifestyle you will benefit from having other positively-oriented people as supporters. Those who similarly hold a clear, strong image of their positive objectives can assist you to maintain your own direction towards a successful lifestyle. Thus the people around you may prove to be a significant resource in promoting your successful lifestyle.

In *Create Inner Strength*, the technique of Affirmation was described for bringing forward the qualities of the heart to build your inner resources. Power Statements work in a similar way, but are directed more towards your outer success, goals and objectives. Again, this is a technique with which you can experiment until you find how it can best serve you.

The idea is to form a verbal image which makes a vivid, positive and powerful impression on your unconscious mind so that your target is dynamic and clear within you. With repetition of your Power Statements, your goal becomes like a beacon, a guiding light towards which you are drawn and directed. The clearer and brighter your vision, the more effectively your inner monitor for success will work.

Even though every step of the way to your goal may not be clearly defined, as it rarely is, you nevertheless can be clear about what you want and are going towards. Then, when you do go 'off course', you will know, before wasting too much time and energy, and can make the necessary adjustments. The more powerful the beacon, or image of success, within you, the better your inner monitor will function, the easier it will be to stay on course for your objectives.

Power Statements – E.A.R.

This is just one approach to creating Power Statements which can strengthen your determination to get to your goal. The letters are a reminder of the structure of the statement:

E Experience
A Action
R Result

These letters may also remind you to listen for your inner guidance, as it is being attracted to you.

E

Firstly, how will you **experience** the process of getting to your goal? What are the most positive qualities associated with working towards your fulfilment? How will you feel on the journey to your chosen destination? Would you like to have more ease, adventure, fun, excitement, pleasure?

A

Secondly, what key **actions** will you be taking? There may be some aspects of travelling to your goal that have a negative side to them – how can they be stated most positively, with greatest encouragement for you? What are the challenges for you associated with the goal? What will you need to *do* differently to bring about the changes you would like? What are the essential steps you will be taking?

R

Finally, what is the **result** or end picture you want to have? What is the goal you are aiming for? What is the beacon you are heading towards?

For this particular exercise, keep the Power Statement as a single statement and distil each E. A. R. to the major points that will have greatest impact for you.

For example:
E It is fun and easy for me
A to encourage and support my team
R in successfully completing our award-winning
documentary film.

E I love
A effecting my healthy and nutritious diet as
R I attain my goal weight of 120 pounds.

E With great confidence,
A I am giving an outstanding audition,
R landing the leading role.

E With pleasure
A I carefully prepare a detailed proposal and
R win the contract for our business.

E I am grateful as
A I learn to listen and develop my intuition
R in promoting the best in myself and others close
to me.

As a next step in this exercise, you might like to experiment with one of your Power Statements. As with Affirmations, repetition imprints the successful image within you. Try then repeating a Power Statement 100 times. A simple way to record your 100 is to take pen and paper and write a stroke for each time you say the Statement. Every 5th stroke can be drawn through a row of 4. 20 groups of 5 strokes take you to the 100. You may find yourself 'switching off' the conscious mind as you repeat the words. Keep going anyway until number 100. Notice now how you feel about your vision.

Power Statements serve to strengthen your commitment to

your goals and reinforce the new positive focus and direction for your energies. For many of us, a successful lifestyle is dependent upon sufficient financial resources, plus a bit more if we can have it. We are surrounded by many mixed messages about money. Do you recognize any of the following?

- Good people do not have a lot of money.
- Success is not having to work for a living.
- You cannot enjoy life without money.
- You have to be a criminal to be rich.
- There is not enough money in the world to go around.
- Rich people are not really happy.
- Having money is too much responsibility.
- You cannot be rich and spiritual.
- You have made it in the world when you own a Rolls Royce.

It is hard to enjoy an expectation of success when you may be harbouring some of these, or similar, mixed messages about money. Confusion in your beliefs produces confusion in your emotions, and therefore confusion in your results. You may need to stand back from the input you have received so far about money to discover and be clear about what is true for you in your experience so far, and what it is you need and want for yourself now.

Supposing your expectation of success does include increased financial resources. In order to prepare your inner environment for this aspect of your success, you will need to confront, address and eliminate any beliefs that would negate your potential for fulfilment. This is in fact true for any 'increase' in your personal circumstances. Money is one of the simplest ways of demonstrating this principle.

The next point is that if you choose to charge your emotional environment with a certain set of expectations, it is most important that you actively channel your energy towards producing the outcome. Not doing so would be like failing to fulfil an agreement with your self (see the Action/Productivity Cycle) and undermines your well-being. The energies that you build within yourself and do not express have a way of almost 'rotting' inside.

The following exercise may assist you to move beyond any lack of clarity you may have concerning money, into your picture of financial well-being.

My Picture of Financial Success

The two parts of this exercise are firstly, bringing to mind the most powerful experience of fullness, well-being and plenty and secondly, observing freely the material world images that match the positive emotions.

Relax your physical body by breathing deeply and evenly, letting go of any pressures and tensions, mentally, physically or emotionally. Imagine you are by the edge of the ocean, with steady waves breaking on the shore, evenly washing the sand. Envisage yourself sitting comfortably on the beach, peacefully running sand through your toes, a gentle warm wind caressing your face. Smell the salt and breathe the clear air deeply into you.

You notice the grains of sand that stick to your skin and look across the beach to many more millions of grains. You look beyond each wave that breaks in front of you, and see the expanse of ocean that extends further than the eye can see.

In such an ocean, there is so much energy. The energy of currents, the life of plants and animal forms, greater than your imagination can begin to embrace.

Just for a moment, become the ocean, become its power and fullness. Observe within you the natural vitality without stress. There are great riches within you, plenty to sustain you, as much as you could possibly ever hope to have pass through you.

Breathe in deeply once again, and expand that quality of fullness, of well-being, of vitality. Be aware of the peace and relaxation throughout your body. Staying in touch with those qualities, allow to come into your mind the one material asset that matches this experience of ease and fulfilment.

Is there a financial price to pay for this asset? If so, what is

> *it? Bring your conscious attention present now and make any notes you would like about your experience, including the material asset, or assets if there was more than one. You may wish to evaluate consciously your wish to pursue achieving this particular outcome. If you decide that it is important for you, you may wish to add a picture of it to your Treasure Map.*

When you know clearly what you want beyond previous limiting conditions and beliefs, then you may wish to charge your emotional environment with a new picture of financial success. The example below illustrates how a Power Statement assisted someone at a time of hardship to create a new experience of trust within himself, and thus effect a positive change in his material circumstances.

The man in question was in debt and, given his existing financial commitments, could not see a way to repay it. He wrote the following Power Statement, 10 times every day for 30 days. Writing Power Statements is another way of strengthening the impression on your unconscious. The Power Statement he wrote was:

God is my abundant supply and large sums of money come to me easily, under grace and in perfect ways, for the highest good of all.

An important phrase in this Power Statement is 'for the highest good of all'. We may be much more powerful than we currently realize. The death of a loved one close to us might be far too high a price to pay for the temporary relief of a financial problem.

At the end of the month, he was offered £5,000 to do a job he was planning to do voluntarily. He carried on writing out the Power Statement for a further two weeks, at the end of which time his parents decided to give him part of his inheritance of £40,000 to save taxation, which solved his critical problem. Another two weeks writing the Power Statement and he was offered a new job with an excellent salary and package of benefits.

Writing out the Power Statement took him a few minutes each day and it had the effect, emotionally, of lifting him above his level of anxiety, and feelings of need, to knowing that somewhere there was a solution to his problem. His outlook grew more confident so that he noticed and was attracted to positive solutions, rather than negative difficulties.

Similarly, you could use a Power Statement to reinforce your confidence of financial or material success.

There is a spiritual principle of 'tithing' where you give back 10 per cent of all you receive to your church, or an organization that is involved in charitable work. Giving in this way is demonstrating to yourself that you have more than you need. It reflects an attitude of trusting that we live in a world of plenty, and that we can afford to give away a surplus because our needs are always provided. Tithing is an act of faith, as is any expectation of success.

Until you have concrete, tangible results, you cannot know for sure that you are successful by your own definition. People who tithe usually find that their giving is rewarded, not necessarily in financial terms, but in peace of mind, or the qualities that money so often represents to us. However, people often discover that pretending, in tithing, that they have more than they need, results in their actually having more than they need.

An important aspect of expecting success is to bring into your imagination the way you will be experiencing your life, as if you had already accomplished your goal now.

Then **project your expectancy of success . . .**

Live your life now with the frame of mind that you expect to have once your goals are achieved, your inner strengths and qualities already vibrantly in place. Act as if you already have all you need, and more. From one perspective, this is in fact quite true. Within you now, you do have all the resources you need in order to achieve a successful life.

Charging your inner environment with the expectation of success will be one way in which you can communicate to the world around you what you are going for. To project your success, demonstrate yourself as a successful person. Your manner and body language will convey your inner intention.

There may be times when you do not feel quite as confident as you like. If, however, you hold and present yourself as if you were confident, you will not only build your inner sense of confidence, but that will be the impression you give to others. It is rather like a swan swimming on a lake: the serenity on the surface of the lake does not convey the feet energetically paddling away underneath. Similarly, you could have butterflies in your stomach, but nevertheless look calm.

As you project your success, you will radiate your positive expectancy. This means knowing exactly what you want, and fully expecting to get it. When you are radiating your positive expectation, others will be less likely to obstruct you.

It will be as though you are shooting arrows of success out towards your clearly-defined target, so that the world around you also learns, and is confident, of your success in advance of its arrival. This will make any attempts at rejection on your part, or on the part of anyone else, feel out of place.

In fact, you will be making it much easier for others to go along with you, in support of you, because it will cost too much effort to try to stand in your way and block 'the inevitable'. Do all you can to maintain your positive assumption, inwardly and outwardly.

The spoken language you use will also illustrate your inner world of success, both what you say, the specific words you use, and importantly *how* you talk with people. Have you ever noticed that some people have the capacity for saying the most outrageous things, and somehow get away with it because the underlying message is caring and friendly?

The Language Diet

Affirmations and Power Statements consciously impress the unconscious because you take time to focus on them. However, our everyday thoughts and speech are constantly influencing us.

In a survey similar to the one mentioned in *Unlock Your Attitude,* it was observed through the course of a day that toddlers were given 30 negative commands to 1 piece of encouragement. The negatives went along the lines of:

Don't fidget
Keep quiet
Don't talk like that
Don't use that word
Don't do that
Behave yourself
Don't go there

Those kinds of commands may still be running as an undercurrent in our lives, undermining our natural curiosity and creativity, and replacing it with fear and doubt. For the most part, we may be unconscious and unaware of the stream of negative self-thought. We may even have placed a veneer of behaviours over it to conceal it from ourselves and others.

When you eat foods that are 'negative', in the sense that your body does not assimilate them, the result is excessive physical weight on your body. Similarly, thoughts and words which do not positively serve your mind and emotions may cause heaviness in terms of your personal vitality, well-being and peace of mind.

The first part of this exercise is to take a page in a notebook and fill it with a description of your positive qualities. Each statement must be totally positive and without any qualification, such as 'sometimes', 'occasionally', or 'I've known it to happen that . . . '.

For example:

I am a good athlete
I am kind to old people
I am generous
I have a good sense of humour
I am a courageous businesswoman

I love playing tennis
I am very enthusiastic in my work
I am sensitive and a good listener
I enjoy my life
I am a tender lover with my wife
I love meeting new people
I am a good and reliable friend
I am patient and tolerant

It is not necessarily the fact that you have denied any of the qualities you outline, but reminding yourself of your positive attributes will assist you in deleting the unconscious negatives of which you may be presently unaware.

The second part of this exercise is an experiment to conduct for a day, or half a day if you would prefer. The challenge is to view everything about your day in a totally positive light, with every thought and speech having a positive orientation. Not only will you be holding a high positive regard for yourself, but also for everyone and every event that you encounter personally, or hear about via newspaper, TV or radio.

You might choose to eliminate some negative expressions, just for that day.

This could include expressions such as:

It's impossible to . . .
I can't . . .
It can't get any worse
Disasters always happen in threes
It's useless
It's just my luck..
People never get it right
I never was good at . . .
All teachers / businessmen / policemen / politicians demonstrate 'x' negative behaviour . . .
There will never be enough . . .

It's hard for me . . .
It's difficult to . . .
It's bad enough when . . .
It never rains but it pours
I try hard but . . .
Whenever you get anything good, something always comes along to spoil it.

There are many negative tones or inferences that are a part of our common language and limiting expectations. When you spot one within yourself, and express yourself more positively, give yourself a reward. The child within us responds delightfully to praise, rewards and appreciation.

At the end of your day, make some notes about your successes and what you learnt about the times you 'slipped'. How would you address those times differently in the future?

When you have completed your day, give yourself a reward for being willing to undertake and learn from your experiment.

How we regard ourselves is sometimes reflected in how we dress. Are there any changes you would like to make now to your clothing to reflect more accurately your expectation of a successful lifestyle? How might your personal appearance more effectively project your positive expectation? What is the clothing that will best match the ability you are now demonstrating? What colour or style brings out the best in you?

Lack of self-care indicates a lack of interest in, or love of, life. What you wear and how you wear it does not only tell others about your state of mind, it may also tell you about your level of self-respect, something about your level of caring whether or not you and your objectives in life have any value.

Presenting yourself *as if you are already successful* can in itself boost your morale. The care that you take in dressing is just as important for your self-esteem as impressing the world around you. Taking care to raise your self-esteem when you are meeting new challenges may assist you keeping your eyes focused positively on your objectives. Even if your goals do not involve much interaction with others, dress up for yourself once in a while.

Appearances may be deceptive and this can be a very good thing. When you are building your confidence in a new endeavour, your personal presentation is what makes an initial impact on meeting. Other people may make positive assumptions about you based upon how you look. This could give you a head start at a crucial moment, just when it matters most.

With your positive expectation of success fully in mind, you might wish to go through all your cupboards, closets and drawers and discard any clothing (right down to your underwear) that does not reflect the quality of life you now anticipate.

You may already be aware how much we communicate through our 'body language', the way we stand, sit, move and generally hold ourselves. People can see and often feel our state of mind, before we have even said one word. Very direct forms of contact that 'speak' to others are the eye contact you make and the quality of your handshake.

Allow such contact as demonstrates that you are confidently with them, open and receptive to them. A firm handshake conveys the firmness of your intent and establishes you as a person who is worth spending time getting to know better.

In order to project yourself fully you may need to gather some information about your proposed new endeavour, literally sensing yourself within the appropriate environment. Projecting your success, acting as if you were already successful, might be enhanced by, in some cases, literally putting yourself in the driver's seat, getting the feel of the experience in all its dimensions.

This could be like a child pretending he was already an engine driver, or a doctor, or a pop star. A role play can impress the unconscious and make it become even more comfortable with a new experience. Even before you have achieved the result, you believe within you that it has already become a part of your existence.

So, acting as if you are already successful, *do* something to show that you expect the result you are working towards. For example, if you are wanting to buy a Porsche, test drive one, get the feel of it and see yourself in the driving seat. Explore the possibility of ownership for yourself. You will know if this is a dream that is worth your active pursuit into reality, or not. Participating in the action, gaining the experience will serve you with information to assist you to move forward.

If you want to write a novel, make a book in 'mock up' form with the title and your name on the cover. If you are working towards a certificate or qualification, mock one up and write your name on it so that your unconscious begins to assume that result. If you want to become a successful leader in some enterprise, such as running your own business, conduct yourself as though you were already in the role. Read about leadership. What makes a good leader in your eyes? Discover and put into practice the behaviour and level of personal responsibility associated with leadership. What have you learnt directly in your own experience of leaders? What would you do the same, and what differently? How would you bring out the best in other people? How can you fulfil those qualities of leadership in your life now?

If you want to appear on TV, go to television studios and get the feel of that environment and the people who work there. Listen to people who know about the business and find out what you will need to do to succeed in your aim. Find a professional who can help you practise the techniques and skills you will need to be successful.

Venturing up the 'paths to the rose gardens' of your success is a way of 'making friends' with what you want. You are both preparing the frame of mind, and painting the picture within it. The inner reality as you create it will be a part of bringing about the outer reality.

Affirmations, Power Statements and Visualizations are all

enhanced and strengthened by getting all of your senses involved in the new experience being created. The more you can vividly see, feel, hear, touch (inwardly and outwardly), taste and even smell the new level of participation in your life, the more effectively it becomes impressed within you. The more powerful the inner impression, the more your intuition can come into helping you achieve your objectives.

A further technique to employ and utilize the power of your internal imagery in challenging situations is that of a physical 'anchor'. Many of us have mannerisms of some kind, of which we are unaware for the most part. Have you ever noticed people who pull at their chins when they feel shy? There is often an unconscious connection between such mannerisms and the internal makeup. What is more, a person who is feeling uncomfortable inside will 'communicate' the discomfort, no matter what facade he/she presents.

However, by using powerful creative imagery and an anchor, you bring your inner strengths actively into your personal challenges to replace any doubt or fear with confidence. It will be these strengths that are communicated within yourself and to others, and make a positive impression, the impression of assurance you wish to make.

First of all, you need to recognize the power of your creative imagination and know a little better the impact it makes on your inner environment. Imagine sucking on a lemon and notice how your body responds. Or think of chewing on chocolate wrapping foil. Can you imagine the scent of a rose on a warm summer day? Bring to mind the love you have for your child, a dear friend, spouse or lover and notice how that feels inside. What is the most beautiful scene you can bring to mind, such as a sunset, a huge expanse of green countryside, sunrise over a lake, snow-capped mountain peaks. Now think of a sound, the sound of an ocean for example, or a waterfall, the breeze in leafy trees. What are the images for you to imagine with all of your senses that give you the most powerful, positive emotional experience?

At a peak moment of your experience inwardly, you create the physical 'anchor', a reference point which will in future serve to revitalize you with the powerful emotions of your experiential picture of success, built within you. An anchor can be a finger and thumb touching, or rubbing an earlobe, holding your hands a certain way – the more discreet and less obvious the better.

Anchoring for Success

As with other visualization exercises, make yourself as comfortable as possible, relaxed, free from any disturbances so that you can give your full attention.

Take in a deep breath . . . let it go and with it any concerns, anxieties or preoccupations . . . Another deep breath . . . let that go and allow a deep peacefulness to permeate throughout you . . .

Bring to mind an image that is vivid and that you can see very clearly – a scene in nature . . . a favourite room . . . notice in detail the colours and forms of your image . . . Next, bring a sound to mind . . . a bell . . . the sea . . . wind blowing . . . This time, an event . . . or a person . . . whatever . . . whoever . . . brings a deep quality of loving and happiness into you . . . allow the loving to grow and fill you . . . Introduce a taste – something that makes your mouth water . . . ice cream . . . chocolate . . . pineapple . . . mango . . . Finally, imagine . . . a smell that has a powerful, positive association for you . . . a rose . . . pine forest . . . ocean spray . . .

With your senses heightened and alive . . . create your anchor . . . by touching your fingers together . . . or holding your wrist . . . or putting your hand under your chin . . . Inwardly, you have now caught your attention . . . be aware of that inner connection you have . . .

In tune with the power of all your senses . . . bring into your mind . . . into your imagination . . . your success . . . the successful outcome of your goal . . . if it is a new bodyweight . . . see yourself on the scales as they measure that ideal weight . . . feel yourself wearing comfortably the size of clothing that now looks so good on you . . . hear the appreciation of others as they notice how well you look . . . and touch your anchor physically to record your success in your unconscious mind . . .

Or you might feel yourself opening an envelope and pulling out the cheque, written to you with the amount that you need . . . winning a contract for a new piece of business . . . shaking hands with a client . . . skilfully handling a negotiation in which you experience yourself winning . . . as you imagine the success, touch your anchor . . .

Whatever the success is that you envisage, use your imagination to give it as much detail as possible . . . using as many senses as you can . . . and anchor that experience of success within you.

When you are challenged in the world, and need some positive reinforcement, touching your anchor will bring forward the extra strength you need to overcome the obstacle, inner or outer, that might otherwise delay your success.

Win In Your Fantasy

Your unconscious does not really care what you elect to slot into it. Positive or negative, it is all the same. The best way to deal with negative experiences from the past, or negative expectations of the future (fears), is not to dwell on them, or 'feed' them by giving them your attention or emotional input, but to replace them with the desired positive experience of your choice. It is even possible to 'heal' a painful negative experience or memory by choosing the powerful positive outcome that you would have preferred, having that one now replace the former in your unconscious.

For example, as a child you might have experienced a situation in which you were bullied and were not emotionally or otherwise equipped to stand up for yourself. As an adult, you might still hold unconsciously a fear of being bullied, although you could now devise any number of strategies for standing up for yourself. The old negative fear might prevent you from doing so effectively and you still find yourself in different ways being 'bullied' by other people or life circumstances because the pattern is locked in to you.

Using your creative imagination, you could take yourself back to that first childhood experience of being bullied. Then, choose and create, in the present moment, a powerful positive experience within yourself of another scenario, drawing on your adult wisdom and resources to produce the outcome you would have preferred. It is possible to effect profound healings with this technique. This process is one in which you can always *win in your fantasy*.

Winning in your fantasy is one of the most powerful ways of claiming the authority over your life and promoting your successful lifestyle. You no longer need to be subject of the negative influence of past experiences, or others' negative expectations of you from the past. Whether your doubts and fears originate from a previous source, or are adrift in your thinking, you can use the power of your creative imagination to transform the negative experience into a positive one.

This is a very profound choice to make because in one sense you cannot change the facts about the past. You can, however, change the imagery within you if you would like to do so. Supposing you had failed to live up to an unspoken expectation of yourself and had lived with a sense of regret about it, such as not being physically present at the death of a loved one. If you wished, you could envisage the scene taking place differently, with the outcome you would have preferred.

In effect, this is like replacing a negative track with a positive one. Like any objective in life, this must be one you really want and are willing to believe for it to be effective for you. To test how it works, you might first select an experience which has a lesser charge in your life and keep an open mind towards the possibility of the technique working. In the area of belief, if you think something cannot work, you will demonstrate that outcome and be proved correct.

Claiming Authority Over Your
Life – Winning In Your Fantasy

In a literal sense, you are the author of your life. You write the script, unconsciously or otherwise, and play the lead role. However, up to now, you may have felt more like a victim of circumstances than the cause and originator.

To claim the authority that you do in fact have, you will realize your inherent power for transforming any area of limitation. Two of the most limiting emotions you may encounter in progressing towards your objectives may be fear and doubt. These could surface either from similar past experience, or be the product of a good imagination, negatively orientated.

Any fear or doubt that you confront and overcome will release more of your energy to you, even a relatively small fear may be containing more of 'you' than you realize.

If there is some action you wish to undertake but are experiencing fear or doubt towards it, use this exercise to create a positive experience for yourself. For this action, you will now create an experience of winning.

Bring the circumstances of your challenge vividly to mind. Envisage yourself within them, feeling strong and empowered. You might like to breathe in deeply a few times, and if you have a Success Anchor, bring to mind the images of your Anchor, and activate it, however you do that.

Now allow the scene to unfold in the way you would really like it. Envisage yourself confidently acting towards a successful conclusion, where you bring forward your skills and resources to create your win. What are the qualities you are demonstrating to yourself now? You might like to create an Affirmation of these qualities and anchor that affirmation into your winning experience so that you charge the words with strong, positive emotions.

Run the successful scene through your mind a few times,

with your Affirmation and Anchor, so that you feel fully at home with it.

When you approach your challenge 'for real', use your Affirmation and Anchor to reconnect you with your winning fantasy. When you have demonstrated the success to yourself, give yourself acknowledgement and a reward.

For example, supposing you had a fear of diving head first into a swimming pool. Even though the fear is not a major one, it nevertheless holds you back from something you might enjoy. You would take some quiet time to relax and bring to mind some of the qualities that you would need to be successful, such as confidence, calm and ease.

Breathe in deeply, imagining these qualities. Using your Anchor, you would bring forward a strong experience of your capabilities and then envisage yourself taking the action and successfully achieving your result.

Your Affirmation might be:

I am calm, confident and at ease.

You then run the winning scene through your mind, with the Affirmation, and Anchor the experience within you.

When it comes to taking action, you use the Anchor and the Affirmation and take small steps towards building your confidence until you get the result you want.

As you experiment with any of these exercises to reinforce your expectation of success, know that you will be sowing seeds of positivity. Some of these seeds will grow and blossom in the immediate future. Others may seem to lay dormant for a number of years before bearing fruit. Nothing, however, will be lost to you.

Each small positive step counts and will contribute, now or later towards your enrichment. You may even find that you do a written exercise, forget about it for years and then turn it up, to discover that your early vision has already come about. You may not consciously have done anything about it.

Acknowledge, and never underestimate, each small success

on the way to your goal. Rather like counting your blessings, each touch or brushstroke of success contributes its colour to the final picture. There is not just one final success to be measured, but a delightful array of colour and form that fill and complete the art of successful living.

There is a powerful exercise of creating your future Programme For Success, which embraces *all* aspects of your life, particularly the qualities with which you want your life to be enriched.

A preliminary step to writing your Programme For Success is to identify the successful expression and experience of your expanded Comfort Zone, the new preferred habits and behaviours which are your anticipated successful lifestyle.

Your Programme For Success

For the purpose of this exercise, give your imagination full permission to step beyond your normal limits. Allow your dreams to come true! At the same time, choose what you really want for yourself. It is an exercise that is worth playing with more than once, refining it to your liking, until it resonates for you and inspires your greatest enthusiasm.

It may help you to refer back to previous exercises in which you got in touch with all the various aspects that would constitute a successful lifestyle for you. Details here will make this exercise more effective.

You may prefer to write it out in paragraphs or itemize it, whatever way feels most comfortable, easy and has the greatest impact for you. Each statement is powerful, positive and in the present tense, like an Affirmation or Power Statement, so that your imagination impresses the unconscious right now. Remember to incorporate the positive experiences and expressions of your new qualities. What will you successfully be demonstrating to yourself in the process of achieving your objectives? How will your success look, feel, sound – even taste or smell?

For example, this is how an itemized Programme For Success might look:

- I select excellent personnel to work with me on the team
- I make clear, sound and workable agreements with everyone involved
- With encouragement and enthusiasm, I get the best performances out of each individual
- I receive outstanding support from my family and friends
- I am open to and receive extraordinary assistance when confronting challenges
- It is easy for me to find simple solutions at difficult turning points
- Every experience I have serves me in creating success
- I enjoy taking care of small details
- I am persistent in my optimism and self-discipline
- I am grateful for all opportunities that come to me
- I am delighted with the success of the finished product
- I am winning wonderful acclaim in my press reviews
- I am happy and at peace with myself

When you have written your Programme For Success you can either keep it somewhere for referral on a frequent, regular basis, or put it to one side. Above all, keep it confidential to yourself. No one else need know your deepest aspirations and it is better that they do not. Your powerful images of success are part of your personal process and may weaken with disclosure your resolve to fulfil them. Telling others the more personal details of your anticipated success may take away your energy and commitment for following through and actively producing the results.

At a later time, you may wish to write another Programme when you know from your experience how this process best works for you. Meanwhile, you might experiment reading through your Programme For Success, say once a week. You could find that without giving it any further attention, some of the outcomes happen anyway, of their own accord. Sometimes, simply stating the wish to yourself and writing it down is sufficient to have it come about.

However successful you have been in the past, know that there is always more. There are many examples of people who upon concluding their working lives, take on greater challenges or adventures than were available to them earlier on. With each experience of success, you may care to redefine achievement for yourself. With each experience of success, you may discover new areas within yourself, or the world around you, that you want to know better. The chances are that you have plenty of challenges to overcome, talents, qualities and gifts to unwrap, so that your life can become progressively richer and more rewarding.

Few 80-year-olds are seeking achievement in marathon races, although there are a few. In your 80s, you may wish to expand your successful lifestyle along less physically strenuous routes. At any age, life presents us with opportunities for learning, growth and expansion into increased well-being, when we are alive to them.

One of the benefits of growing older is the wisdom gained from life's experience. The disadvantage of such experience is that it may allow us to narrow or limit how we approach life's opportunities. We can potentially bring our creativity and imagination to generate a fresh and optimistic new look at our circumstances as winners, generating the best possible experience out of any condition.

At the different stages of your life, you may wish to review the elements of a successful lifestyle in the light of your age, education, personal development, wisdom. If you are building your career in your 20s and 30s, your success will be measured in those terms. If you are bringing up children and running a home, there is also personal success to be appreciated, although time and space to do so may be limited. In your 40s or 50s, you may be redefining your career or vocational aims so that you draw more fully on your work experience and expertise to date. Increasing numbers of people are achieving a peak of occupational fulfilment in their 70s.

If your deepest motivation were being fulfilled now, how would your successful lifestyle look? What is the highest good that you could possibly be aiming for? What is the greatest value you can fulfil?

What if you could operate in partnership with whatever represents your highest good, your greatest possible expression and experience in life? That partnership would be bringing you your most intense level of satisfaction, your greatest success.

This next exercise can assist you in drawing on your deepest resources and receiving further guidance from within. As with any advice you receive, make sure you know how you can make practical use of it.

Sometimes advice may come in symbolic form so you may not want to take its meaning at face value. You may be given leads or indications that take you indirectly to your next step. The suggestion to go and collect flowers may mean just that; to enhance your workplace with flowers, for example. It could also mean to take stock of your own value, where 'flowers' represent your qualities.

Working With Your Highest Good

Take some undisturbed time to be with yourself, relax in a comfortable chair and if you like, put on some soft, relaxing music.

Breathe deeply . . . let that go and let go of any concerns or

*anxieties . . . breathe deeply again, breathing in peacefulness
. . . and breathe out any physical tensions, aches or pains . . .
Observe your breathing now . . . Just feel it . . .*

*Observe your everyday life now . . . the matters that absorb
your attention in the course of applying yourself . . . Allow
yourself to take off the involvements of your personality . . .
like taking off your clothes . . . and enjoy the freedom that
comes to you . . .*

*Bring to your mind a point of bright white light . . . breathe
into it . . . and watch it expand and grow until it surrounds
and swirls around you . . .*

*As this light moves . . . allow it to bring a scene which
represents your highest good . . . you may be doing an
exceptional task in ordinary circumstances . . . or an ordinary
task in unusual circumstances . . . where your reward is deep
satisfaction . . . and others benefit from your contribution . . .*

*Entering this scene is a figure . . . the guide to your highest
good . . . Your guide has infinite resource . . . At any time
when you need assistance . . . you have only to ask . . . and
you will receive inspiration . . . encouragement . . . words of
wisdom . . . gifts . . . comfort . . . reassurance . . . direction
. . . clarification . . . the next steps to take . . .*

*Your guide now has a gift for you . . . one that is wrapped
. . . that you receive and open . . . With immense gratitude
. . . you take the gift and notice what it represents for you . . .
now . . .*

*You thank your guide and ask if there is any information that
they have for you . . . listen for their response . . . when the
time is right, allow the figure to fade back into the scene of light
. . . And know that in any moments of darkness . . . you can
always return to this scene of light . . . and your guide . . .
when you have the need . . . your guide will always support
you towards your greatest success . . .*

*Gradually and in your own timing . . . become once again
aware of your surroundings . . . get up and stretch.*

In a journal or notebook, write down any details of your

experience with your guide, the information you received, how you might apply that information in your life, the gift and what it meant for you.

When you achieve your successes, remember to celebrate them. Let others be a part of your success, let them enjoy not necessarily the material fruits but your spirit or essence of success. As you demonstrate yourself to be a winner in your life, you give others confidence and courage also to win because you may show that what was seemingly impossible is in fact real for you. Remember that success is a process of expansion once you positively take charge of your life. You may know the phrases:

Success attracts success
Success breeds success

The clouds above us join and separate,
The breeze in the courtyard leaves and returns.
Life is like that, so why not relax?
Who can stop us from celebrating?

The Tao of Pooh
Benjamin Hoff

Chapter 6
Simply Have Fun

Whatever the circumstances of your life to date, you might like to remind yourself that:

It is never too late to have a happy childhood.

Nadine Stair of Louisville, Kentucky, wrote this at the age of 85:

If I had my life to live over . . .

I'd dare to make more mistakes next time.
I'd relax. I would limber up.
I would be sillier than I have been this trip.
I would take fewer things seriously. I would take more chances.
I would take more trips.
I would climb more mountains and swim more rivers.
I would eat more ice cream and less beans.
I would perhaps have more actual troubles,
but I'd have fewer imaginary ones.

You see, I'm one of those people
who live sensibly and sanely hour after hour, day after day.
Oh, I've had my moments
and if I had it to do over again,
I'd have more of them.
In fact, I'd try to have nothing else.
Just moments, one after another,
instead of living so many years ahead of each day.

What if life was simple? What if life was fun? Could you imagine your life where enjoyment was the main feature, and not just the intermission?

In this chapter, we shall be drawing on some of the wonder and awe, glee and delight of the child-like world within us. We may never have had all the fun we could with these qualities as children, and the chances are that the demands of our adult lives have cast them into shadows. Hand in hand with the logical, step-by-step progression towards our aims we can enjoy playing with techniques which are better understood by the inner child.

Your inner child may give you the most direct route, even if it is not the most 'logical'. He or she will respond well when you have moments of fun. Of course, you as the adult always have the final say and will make a conscious decision as to how to act, or what to do.

Angels can fly because they take themselves lightly.

Scottish Saying

You have probably noticed how easy it is to get up to do something you really enjoy doing, such as meeting a special friend, playing tennis, planning a holiday, horseback riding, going to a favourite sporting event. Little effort is involved. With enthusiasm for the activity, you may lose track of time as you are spontaneously absorbed in what you are doing.

Successful living might be the result of streamlining your life so that your choices of attitude and activity give you the maximum return of enjoyment. So far, you may have identified a number of objectives and goals you felt you wanted to pursue. You may also be aware that there are some conflicts in what you want.

When the 'wants' you have are in conflict, your energy will be drawn in different directions and the result can be a lack of fulfilment in one or more of them. The conflicts would be for example wanting to enjoy the demanding role of motherhood while pursuing a career in the City. Or wanting a fulfilling marriage, while pursuing sex and romance with other partners. Or wanting to study to become an astrophysicist while spending hours working out in the gym. Or wanting to create a financial empire while pursuing an academic career. It is possible that in the course of your lifetime, you may accomplish two disparate aims, but not necessarily at the same time.

Right now, it is likely that one of your conflicting 'wants' has a stronger sense of importance, a greater priority and therefore will produce greater fulfilment. This next exercise will assist you to examine and explore potential directions and then identify which has greatest meaning for you.

Eliminating Your Lesser Wants

The first step is, with a pad of paper and pen, and without censoring yourself, to write out all your possible wants, item by item, given a set of circumstances in which you can have anything at all that you could possibly want. In the past, the fear of personal rejection may have prevented you from getting in touch with all of your heart's desires. Put any such fears aside now, and ensure that no one else will be reading what you write. Give your imagination a free rein and do not censor any whim that might come to mind.

In order to relax for this exercise, you may wish to put on a favourite piece of music or sit in a favourite chair. Above all, be comfortable with yourself. Give yourself plenty of time, and more than one sitting if you would like. As the wants surface, allow your imagination to take you into those experiences, as if you already had them.

Note which of those wants have the strongest appeal to you. With those, expand your imagination to embrace all of your five senses. So with each powerful imagined want, ask yourself:

1. How does this look for me? What can I see here?

2. What sounds are associated with this picture? What can I hear?
3. How do I feel in this situation? What sensations, inwardly and outwardly, do I have?
4. Are there any smells that I am aware of?
5. What can I taste?
6. What is the maximum fulfilment for me in this experience?

By this time, you will have noticed which are your 'lesser wants' and you may wish to eliminate them. That is not the only choice you have. If you are not ready to discard them, put them on a back burner, to incubate until such time as you wish to pursue or let them go. You might like to keep a page in a file or notebook of Maybe-One-Day Goals.

Now review your powerful wants by making a separate list of them. This is still within the scope of your imagination and not yet time to make final choices or commitments.

On a scale of 1 to 10, rate each powerful want on the level of expansion you experience with it. 'Expansion' would be an increase in the qualities you most value, or have most meaning for you; qualities such as excitement, enthusiasm, challenge, peace of mind, harmony, loving, pleasure, well-being, vitality.

Are any of your highly rated, powerful wants in apparent conflict? You might take a page for each one, divided with a left column for the negatives or downsides of your want; a right column for the pluses or advantages to you. Making decisions and clear productive choices is not always easy for us because there can be a certain excitement, tension and sense of drama in being pulled in different directions.

The difficulty may arrive when you come to sacrifice the lesser experience in order to pursue the greater. To experience passion in a career, you would sacrifice distractions such as playing golf in the afternoons. To experience passion in a marriage, you would sacrifice the 'exits' from that relationship such as alternative romances, or a lot of activities from which your spouse is excluded. These choices do take courage.

For the purpose of this exercise, experiment and choose the experience of greatest value and enjoyment to you. Make your choice as much as you can in a clear direction towards your maximum fulfilment. Keep in mind that any decision you make will ultimately benefit you with greater personal understanding, one way or another.

Once you have clarified for yourself a positive direction leading to maximum potential fulfilment, you are a step nearer creating a simpler life for yourself. You may encounter many opportunities to be distracted from your main purpose. However, within you is a reference point that can assist you in re-affirming a clear choice. Within you, you know better now what course of action will be rewarding for you, and which less so.

Simplifying what you want to do, and your chosen fields of activity, is one step towards increased enjoyment and success. Not only are you choosing the activity with the maximum return for you, but also you are eliminating the distractions of less fruitful pursuits.

Perhaps one of the greatest art forms we can learn is that of producing the experience of enjoyment when, in order to fulfil a commitment, we must undertake a task for which we have little appetite.

Your unconscious will have negative imagery that represents the task. By using the form of a symbol, you can gain information about your reluctance and then create some new options for yourself. More importantly, the unconscious can also offer you those alternative views of the task, the approaches that will give you a new perspective and more enjoyment.

If you can look forward to an event with anticipation, rather than reluctance, you can improve your experience of it at the time. Change your perception and you may change your experience.

Transforming Your Negative Imagery – Pictorial Diagrams

In the first chapter, we used pictorial diagrams as a way of finding out more about what motivates you. This type of exercise can also be used as a step towards transforming a negatively-charged task or event.

As before, take a pad of paper and a pen and this time draw, in a figurative, symbolic form, without using letters, words or numbers, the event or task, with which you have associated reluctance: fear, doubt or anxiety. An example of this is given in Figure 5.

When you have completed the drawing (remember, you do not need to be a Michelangelo here) ask yourself what the symbol, or symbols, mean for you. When you have the information from that drawing, tear up the drawing and throw it away.

Now with a clean piece of paper, draw, symbolically again, how you would most like to experience that event or task. How could you positively have more enjoyment with it? Allow yourself to be very spontaneous here. An example of this is given in Figure 6.

What does this new symbol mean for you? What do you particularly notice about it? How can you translate it into a new attitude or action? Is there anything you need to communicate to yourself, or anyone else, about this new view? Are there any changes you would like to make in your home or workplace to support this new imagery? Remember to be gentle with yourself.

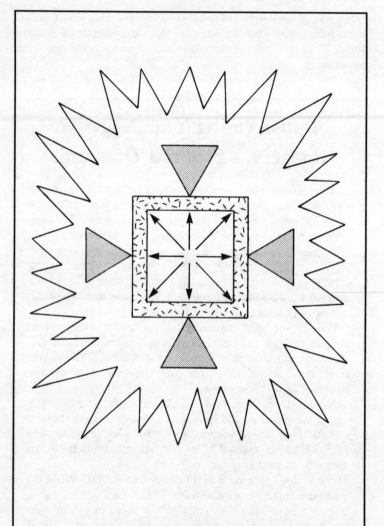

Figure 5: This symbol represents the task of going to an authority figure, such as a bank manager, feeling trapped and powerless (in a box) and being confronted and threatened.

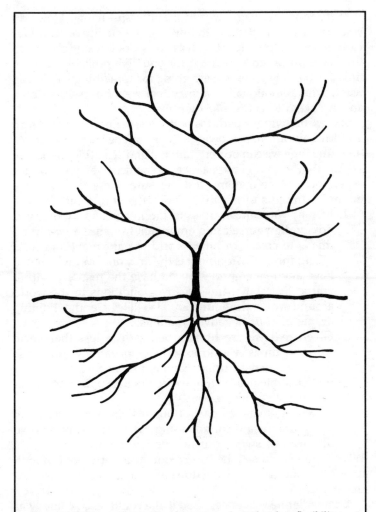

Figure 6: This symbol is like a growing plant that has flexibility and movement. It draws nourishment from the air and the ground. Its environment is friendly and life-supporting. Although the task may be unappealing, it can be 'growth-producing' and expansive with this perspective.

Attitude is the magic word for successful living. How can you simplify your attitude to improve the quality of your life? How can you keep a light touch as you work towards objectives that have power and meaning for you? We probably all have times, especially when we are going for something we deeply want, when emotionally we may feel we let ourselves down and we seem to get in our own way.

Successful living is perhaps both an art and a science. As an art form, our approach towards living can be very creative. At the same time we can be very rational and scientific so that we set up the best of circumstances in which we can produce experiences of enjoyment and pleasure. How then can we minimize troughs of negativity or, better still, avoid them?

1. Ideally, you can set up your life in such a way that you do not dig yourself into emotional troughs. A way to do this is to create an inner world of enjoyment and fun.

    Your inner environment is the only one over which you have any real control. You do have the resource within you to live above any negative conditions in the world around you. Humour can also alleviate the limiting drama of your negative emotions.

2. Given that we are human beings in a less than ideal world at times, we do experience negativity. For those times, we benefit from maintaining a sense-of-humour trigger, strategies, so that we do not take ourselves or our circumstances too seriously.

    We can create, as part of our resources for successful living, the means for accessing our sense of humour so that we can switch our moods into enjoyment.

What if you could see the funny side, recognize the humour, in every condition and circumstance that might otherwise upset you?

A comedienne was once asked if she could teach comedy as a technique for actors. She responded saying that she had attempted to teach comedy at one of London's main drama schools but found that it could not be taught. She recommended to simply keep looking at the funny side of life.

This next exercise is one to practise in your life for a day, or half a day if you would prefer. It is a step towards strengthening your inner world of enjoyment and fun.

Seeing the Funny Side of Life

You may already be aware from your own life, or from doing some of the previous exercises, that what you choose to focus upon is what you attract to you.

To get the best results from this exercise, you will need to prepare yourself in advance. The evening before your chosen day, preferably last thing at night, just before you go to sleep, do the following guided visualization to touch into your inner resources of humour.

Breathe in deeply a few times, and relax your body . . . Let the events of the day fade . . . become quiet with yourself . . . and observe now the easy flow of your breath . . . As you relax.. become aware of your heartbeat.. and observe it . . .

Bring a smile to your face . . . and experience the peace and detachment of being you . . . away from the dramas and concerns of your everyday life . . . just you with the creative spirit of your life within you . . . In your own inner world . . . you can now awaken even more fully to the pure joy that is bubbling inside . . . the joy that is your freedom to be playful . . . to be in the world . . . but not of it . . . Because you are free to create any experience you wish . . . This is your world . . . and your choice . . .

Call on the child within you . . . let him/her know that tomorrow you are going to play together . . . that you will find many situations which are very funny . . . that even if something goes wrong.. you will find something to laugh about . . . Feel the sparkle and glee of your inner child as he/she begins to anticipate a fun day ahead . . .

Now, bring to mind an Affirmation that evokes the quality of fun in you . . . It might be something like:

I am seeing the funny side of life today
or simply,

> *I am fun*
> *and envisage yourself in that frame of mind as you repeat it*
> *a few times within you . . .*
> *. . . just before you go to sleep.*
> *When you wake the next morning, refresh your inner world*
> *of enjoyment with your Affirmation and touch into your sense*
> *of fun. As you go out into your day, be aware of every*
> *opportunity to experience the fullness of pleasure and*
> *enjoyment.*

The last exercise was about setting your inner world to expect enjoyment in the course of your day. You may be a person who laughs easily and for whom life is, in the main, a pleasure. However if you are someone who suffers periodically from a 'sense of humour failure', when life weighs heavily, you might learn from some of the talented comedians who have developed their capacity for humour out of a deep personal need.

Many comedians are sensitive people who have grown up in an environment that was in some way challenging, even hostile, to them. Making others laugh was a way they could gain acceptance in the group and survive emotionally, sometimes physically. If you would like more enjoyment out of life, find out how you can promote it in others.

Humour is positively infectious. Have you ever experienced laughter, passing through a large room of people, like an ocean wave with a rippled surface, when there is nothing particularly to laugh about? Laughter can simply generate its own momentum.

Have you ever had a day strewn with disasters? The plumbing let you down badly; someone ran into the back of your car; the cat was sick over your newly cleaned carpet; you spilt coffee on your new white jacket. A few months later, you may have laughed heartily telling a friend about those events, and your reactions to them.

Some of your most memorable days on holiday, in

retrospect, might have been those when nothing went according to plan. Transportation was horrendous; you were held up for days at the airport because of a strike, taxis broke down in the middle of nowhere, you ended up thumbing a lift on a donkey. Accommodations were fraught with ancient and lethal electrical wiring, uncertain plumbing and ferocious insects and the local deity had his revenge on your digestive system.

Often such adventures are funny in hindsight. However, how could you recognize the humour, at the moment of impact? If it is to be funny later, how might it be funny now?

You might like to find ways of immersing yourself in humour: listen for it in other people, on the radio, television, in books; collect and tell jokes; watch comic videos and films. Generating humour around yourself is an active process, one in which your senses are alert and trained to observe life, not just superficially, but for the unusual, the quirks.

You will need both the facility for a keen perception, and then the creative inner response of picking up the less obvious interpretation of events. Your enjoyment will increase with your capacity to participate fully, and uncritically, in whatever is going on, in and around you.

You may be at a turning point in life, wondering about a fulfilling occupation that is a little different. Did you know that there is a French woman who hires herself out as a professional Laugher? Charging by the hour, she comes with a guarantee to make you laugh.

Norman Cousins, in *Anatomy of an Illness*, describes the healing power of laughter in his recovery from a life-threatening illness. The story goes that he had been experiencing a lot of negative stress in a job, which, as he saw it, led to his illness. He was given a short time to live and powerful medications to ease his pain. A lay reader of the *Lancet*, he recognized the destructive side-effects of his medications. With a doctor sympathetic to his views, he asked to be taken off the medications.

He reasoned to himself that if negative emotions had contributed towards his illness, the positive emotion of humour might help his healing. In place of the medications, he prescribed for himself large doses of vitamin C and 4 hours of laughter a day. He watched all his favourite comedy films. The first benefit he received was an easing of his pain and the ability to sleep better at night. A side-effect was that his laughter created some disturbance in the hospital ward.

So he discharged himself from hospital and went to stay in a hotel with his humorous books, films and cassettes, and the facility of private nursing. The happy ending of the story was that he survived, having learnt how laughter had contributed towards his healing. Humour and laughter promoted his health and longevity, as perhaps they can for all of us.

If laughter is a healer, it is also a teacher. When we can laugh at ourselves and at our mistakes, relaxing our self-criticisms in the process, we become open and receptive to learning. Our fears, concerns and other limiting emotions dissolve. With a certain detachment and objectivity, we can become aware of new approaches available to us. Instead of feeling stuck, with laughter we become free, even care-free. Rather like taking a walk in the fresh air while debating a problem in our minds, laughter gives us a refreshing break and a new perspective.

There is a personal development consultant who offers a service as a Joyologist. She encourages her clients to make their evolvement of growth and expansion as enjoyable as possible. Perhaps one of the greatest challenges we sometimes have is rationally knowing what to do, and emotionally resisting our better knowledge, limiting ourselves to less than our best attitudes and action. Entertainment and laughter can be very effective in assisting us to transform our limiting attitudes into the experience of successful living.

What if entertainment could be an integral part of the school curriculum? Could you imagine schoolrooms alive with the sound of laughter? Joy and enthusiasm could be the best medium for education. The Latin origin of the word education is *e-ducare*, meaning leading out from within. Joy and enthusiasm are qualities that are inherent within all of us. As we open our channels of joy and enthusiasm, we also become receptive to new information that is in alignment with our inner knowing.

Children have a lot to teach us in the use of our imagination to overcome or release blocks, to be free in spirit, having the simplest circumstances become a source of entertainment. They sometimes have a way of waking up the sleeping child inside of us by inviting us into their world. With spontaneity and naughtiness, they will intuitively know how to shatter the order of our crystallized routines, challenge our little weaknesses and limitations and provoke a matching response from us.

Simply Have Fun might be a prayer from the child deep within us:

● to rebel against rules and self-imposed limitation
● to risk adventure
● to explore and reveal
● to discover and disclose
● to dare to live differently

A child's world is often rich with make-believe. A cardboard box can become an ocean liner; a stick, a magic wand; a stone endowed with problem-solving qualities. The forces of good and bad are a source of excitement; fairy tales, monsters and demons, a source of entertainment. Some of the best games involve having to pretend.

An example of this was the family of children whose daily household task was to do the washing up at dinner time. They transformed the chore into an exciting adventure by imagining that the plates they washed were flying saucers. History does not relate whether any of the flying saucers had crash landings. Are there any tasks that you could transform with a change of outlook?

As adults, we can still pretend. With Affirmations and Power Statements, we are pretending a set of circumstances are real for us, in advance of them becoming so. Perhaps at times we seem to benefit from hardship in life, from complexity, confusion, lack of joy. Where we have the choice however, we might benefit more from fun, ease and simplicity. This next exercise is a game of make-believe.

Simply Have Fun – Pretend

For this exercise, you will be putting to one side your rational, limiting mind. With any perceived problem, apparent difficulty or challenge, you will be allowing your child within to create a new reality for you. Do not be concerned how you will bring into effect the new reality, or even if you ever will do so. This is just a game. Give yourself permission to play freely and spontaneously with it.

Whatever the challenge is that you are currently facing, complete one of the three following statements, whichever seems most appropriate.

It's fun for me to . . .
It's easy for me to . . .
It's simple for me to . . .

The next step of the exercise is also outside of your rational, thinking mind. Allow the child within you to be as daring, free, comic or shocking as he/she wants. The next statement to make spontaneously after one of the three above is:

And the way I can do it is . . .

and come up with as many ways as you can.

Even though this is a game, you may come up with valuable ideas. If so, make a note of them, and of when you will experiment with putting them into practice.

With the power of your imagination, you can transform the ordinary into the extraordinary. Not only may a task take on a completely new meaning, but also an environment, especially the work environment in which you may spend eight or more hours a day, could become more interesting.

There was a story told about a tollbooth operator on the Oakland-San Francisco Bay Bridge. His work was more like a 'party'. Between taking the money from passing motorists, he entertained himself, dancing energetically to music.

In comparison, the other tollbooths were like vertical coffins, in which the operators entered alive, to 'die' of boredom for eight hours a day, performing a meaningless task, and emerged to live once again.

The difference for the one who stood out was that his purpose in life was one day to become a dancer. He viewed the administration building nearby and his bosses as paying for his training. What was more, he had a corner office with glass on all sides. He could see the Golden Gate, San Francisco and the Berkeley Hills. Millions of people pay to go on holiday for those views. He just strolled in every day and practised dancing.

Transforming Your Workplace Into a Fun Palace

What can you do to transform *your* workplace into a fun palace?

You may need to do no more than change your outlook in the light of the new direction you are choosing for your life.

Familiarity, routine and an attitude of 'this is the way things must appear' can produce the experience of boredom.

Move furniture, change pictures, plants, flowers. Start making small changes. Take a slow route home from work. Arrive late and skip lunch. Treat those you work with to ice cream one day. Make enjoyment a priority for you, and see how you can infect others. Change the order in which you do your work. Surprise yourself and others with the unusual.

How can you dare to do things differently? How can you turn work into an adventure, and a process of

---

discovery, even for one day? How can you bring your inner world of current work more into alignment with your visions of a successful lifestyle?

You might reflect on the changes you could make. Then choose one day as an experiment to live differently, and be open to continue the experiment more fully in the future.

As human beings, we have the great gift of imagination which we could enjoy more fully. Almost any task can be transformed, with an element of creativity, into one that is experienced as fulfilling.

The following example demonstrates an unusual view of a work scene which brought about an improved level of work performance. The mundane job of maintaining a ship's engines was given the quality of a life-saving mission, where the engines were seen as the vital organs of a human body, and the engineers viewed themselves as skilled surgeons. They wore green surgeon's overalls and had 'Dr' written by their names on locker doors. This took a willingness to play, and make light of what might otherwise have been routine and repetitive work. Any job, any experience, can be fun if we can set ourselves in that frame of mind.

If we can, as far as possible, sail through in a happy frame of mind with what we currently have to deal with, the objectives we are pursuing will find us more easily.

Have you noticed how attractive people are when they are enjoying themselves? That is attractive, in the literal sense of the word. How much easier it is if we can attract to ourselves whatever it is we need in order to progress towards a goal or aim. The quality of enjoyment is magnetic. People who are enjoying themselves are relaxed and radiate a well-being that others are attracted to and want to share. If you are in any sense a 'salesperson', selling or promoting any product or service, people are more likely to buy. How wonderful to be able to attract the results we want in life, and reduce the pain of effort, anxiety and frustration.

As adults, perhaps we lose something of the innocence of play as our games are more highly charged with the need to win, to gain love, or with fears of losing. Considerations such as mortgage payments, the approval of our peers, the need to prove ourselves may inhibit us. The freedom and innocence of play at any age is irresistible and is very appealing. The jester or the clown penetrates our barriers and transcends our resistances.

Spontaneity and freedom connect us to the child within us. The act of prayer is often conducted in a kneeling position, when we humble ourselves and we bring ourselves closer to a child's height. Like a child that has yet to learn how to control and manipulate his/her environment, in prayer we look in simplicity to the assistance of a higher source or inspiration. The methods for achievement offered by our rational minds may sometimes be too limited and insufficient for our vision. We need to look beyond what is immediately at hand, what we currently know and have experienced.

Sometimes it takes a significant crisis before we discover the act of prayer and literally fall on our knees for help. Then we may begin to find the abundance of resource available to supply our needs, whatever they may be. Prayer might be seen as a direct appeal from the child within us to our higher source of wisdom and intuitive knowing. When we have a clear vision of what we want, and ask for the guidance as to how we may go about getting it, the answers may come in many unexpected forms. The first step is to ask, and then to listen and receive what is presented to us.

Affirmations and Power Statements work like the process of prayer. There are other techniques which employ the same principle of drawing on your inner resources for increased fulfilment. Simplicity is a key here. If you have too much on the go, or try to outsmart yourself, you may lose the inner connection. Know also that if you do not get the response you are asking for, your higher wisdom may be offering a blessing in disguise. In hindsight, we may be grateful that some of our prayers are not answered.

Suspend your disbelief and for the purpose of the next exercises, entertain the possibility that . . .

. . . miracles do happen

. . . dreams do come true

. . . and you *can* believe in the magic of your dreams . . .

In previous chapters, the idea of intuition and your increased ability to respond to your resources of wisdom, inner guidance and 'hunches' have been mentioned. Here we will explore intuition more fully.

Your personal resource of intuition is one of your most powerful assets, not in the way of being forceful in the material sense. The intuition needs relaxation, time and space for you to tune in to it, and most importantly, listen for the response. The internal noise of a busy, worrying mind shields you from hearing clearly the 'still, small voice' of your wisdom. This intuitive mechanism within you might be called your **hunchpower** (HP).

When you learn to listen to it, your HP may take you in directions you had never previously considered. You may find yourself spontaneously taking off in ways that surprise you, enjoying a freedom of approach that lightens the dullest of days.

Your innate HP might have little value for you if you perceived the world as being short of resource, short of places your intuition might lead you. However, if this were your attitude, open your mind to the possibility that we live in an extraordinarily rich world; wealthy in terms we cannot begin to imagine. Given that your objectives (in the Personal, Interpersonal and Material areas) are sufficiently important to you, your HP will prove an asset in leading and guiding you. This next exercise will assist you in recognizing and utilizing this precious gift.

Discovering Your Hunchpower

This exercise is one of setting yourself a small achievable goal, then allowing yourself to be guided inwardly towards it. By experimenting with less significant aims, you will discover how your HP operates and then be able to work with it more effectively with larger targets.

Looking first of all at a Personal Goal area, supposing you were aiming to give up smoking. One of the ways you might support yourself doing this might be to go to non-smoking places. Having identified this as a target, you might find yourself being drawn to places, such as restaurants, transport, even private homes, where non-smoking was requested.

Similarly, if you were looking for a form of meditation that would help you to relax, you might find yourself being drawn to articles in the press, hearing about classes being given, or even overhearing someone talking about a technique that was particularly good for people who have difficulty concentrating.

With this exercise, notice how a serendipity takes place. For some 'reason' you find yourself taking a certain direction with a sense of conviction and end up with the result you wanted without having had to work it out in your mind.

In the Interpersonal area, you might identify a need as part of a community service project, such as finding blankets to give to the elderly. With that idea in mind, you may find yourself being attracted to a number of sources of blankets to fulfil the need. Or in a family relationship, the need to create more shared interests and shared time among a group of people with very different aptitudes. Your HP can take you to a solution where you thought none existed, provided you are clear and want enough the outcome.

Perhaps some of the easiest ways in which to discover your HP come in the Material area of goals and objectives. You want to cut down the time it takes you to get to work. Your HP can direct you intuitively to a new route or routes. You want to redecorate a room in a

style and your HP will guide you to the kinds of
magazines to research your idea, and the kinds of stores
that stock what you need.

The greatest challenge in this exercise, and throughout
the book, is knowing clearly enough what you most
want. Once you have clarified your inner vision, your
intention, you may find that the world, almost literally,
falls at your feet with what you want. This is not to say
that you hide in a corner waiting for the goodies to arrive.
However, acting with enthusiasm on your inner
guidance may produce remarkable results for you.

Do this exercise with the following steps:

1. Bring to mind a goal, or some aspect of a goal that
   you are currently pursuing.
2. What is the next immediate resource that would
   most assist you in taking a next step with this goal?
3. Write this down clearly on a sheet of paper as a
   statement.

   For example:

   > I need a title for the play I am writing *or*
   > I am looking for a person who has accounting
   > skills to assist me with my books *or*
   > I would like to find a really good coach who can
   > teach me how improve my game of tennis *or*
   > I need some inspiration for tackling this
   > business problem.

4. Over the next few days, with your quest in the back
   of your mind, allow your HP to guide you. If you
   get an inner nudge to go somewhere without quite
   knowing why, follow it if you can. You may find that
   your needs are often supplied in ways that are very
   unexpected. Your HP could well give you short cuts
   in time and energy that you would never have
   thought about.
5. When you receive your response, find a small way
   to express your gratitude for it, to give something

> back to the world which supplies your needs in sometimes miraculous ways. You might do a favour unexpectedly for a friend; phone someone who would welcome hearing from you; send a donation to a favourite charity.

It is possible that in the course of going for your objectives, you identify a need which seems out of your reach and presents itself as a problem. There may be a specific piece of equipment that you need but do not know how to find in your locality. You may need a resource in terms of a person with certain skills to work with you. Or you may need some information, a book, a technique to deal with an issue, an answer to some difficulty which has been bothering you, the next step in resolving an issue, or even locating a person you have not seen recently.

This next exercise draws on your HP when you are wanting something very clear and specific. Have you ever 'slept on a problem' and found that on waking, you knew what to do?

I Wonder . . .

Wonder is a child like quality of openness in which you keep yourself available to any suggestion, however unreasonable.

On an index or record card, write the words:

'**I wonder how it is possible for me to . . .**' and complete the sentence with the solution you are seeking.

The request needs to be as straightforward as possible. Keep your requests simple, and one at a time. Do not put yourself on overload.

For example:

- I wonder how it is possible for me to . . . meet up again with the man I met on the train to Oxford last week.
- I wonder how it is possible for me to . . . find a person who can assist me overcome my fear of heights.
- I wonder how it is possible for me to . . . discover my next step in identifying a new occupation for myself.
- I wonder how it is possible for me to . . . find a part-time secretary with the level of skills I need.
- I wonder how it is possible for me to . . . adjust my attitude to appreciate my current circumstances.

Read the card through last thing at night before sleeping so that the 'I wonder' statement is the final impression you leave with your HP. You may even find some answers coming to you in your dreams. Repeat the exercise of reading that statement through last thing at night for the next three nights.

During the days, forget about the statement and go about your life with as open and attentive a frame of mind as you can.

Finally, remember to thank **and reward** your HP for its assistance.

A final technique in this section involves the idea of sowing and harvesting. To work this technique, you may need to adopt a certain detachment towards money because it involves placing a monetary value on the outcome you desire, even when the outcome may have no obvious monetary value.

In this technique, the connection between money and value is the emotional content we hold within us, or place out on the objective. In a sense, you calibrate your emotional content with a financial figure. To take perhaps an absurd example, what would be the financial figure in value that you might place on wishing to be a grandparent, on having a grandchild? This might be too emotional a subject for you to be able to even contemplate a comparable figure, if you are very keen to become a grandparent.

Think about some of your inner objectives, such as a better relationship with a child or parent; the quality of freedom in your life; peace of mind. Allow your intuition to come up spontaneously with a sum of money that would represent your objective. There is no good or bad figure. This is just information for your own personal use. If you had that sum of money, you could not 'buy' the inner objective. However, knowing the value you may be placing on an outcome may clarify for you the importance it has for you and encourage you to pursue it more actively.

To take another route on the same idea, the next time you have an ache or a pain, see if you can calibrate it on a scale between 1 and 10, where 1 is hardly any pain at all and 10 is 'take me to the hospital, I think I am dying'. You could similarly calibrate positive feelings, such as your degree of fulfilment right now, on a scale from 1 to 10.

In assessing the worth of a certain outcome, you may place a monetary figure on an emotive value. There may of course be certain tangible objectives, such as a car, clothing, holiday or a job/salary which have a clear monetary tag to them. The Seeding Exercise which follows can be well applied to both inner and outer objectives.

Making the Seed

Form a clear, steady and vivid picture in your mind . . . of the condition (such as a fulfilling relationship, good health or rewarding work), or object you desire.

Be very careful in selecting the details of your picture, because your subconscious mind that will receive it is sharply accurate . . . and you will get the exact replica of what you envisage.

Put the old condition (unhappy relationships, disease or financial stress) out of your mind entirely . . .

Clearly see, feel, hear, touch and taste the new desired state.

Paint the picture carefully inside your head . . . and hold it clearly without wavering or changing your mind . . .

Act then, as if you had already received the condition for which you asked . . . Your manner and attitude would therefore reflect 'fulfilment', 'peace of mind', 'relaxation', 'enthusiasm' . . . whatever the nature of your new condition . . .

Feel it already with the love and joy or whatever positive emotion you would experience, as if it were so . . .

Act it out . . . behave towards your loved ones as though the relationships were already perfectly fulfilling for you; feel the fullness and gratitude of the financial resources that come through the satisfaction and reward of your work; get up and get going, as much as you can, as if you are already enjoying excellent health . . .

For this subconscious mind is like a child . . .

It loves pictures and games and will respond also to any emotional surge you project to it . . .

Now place a monetary value on your desired outcome. What is it worth to you? What does it cost in financial terms?

If the desired outcome were your harvest, what financial seed would you sow to bring about that harvest? This seed figure might be as little as $\frac{1}{100}$ of the monetary value you identified or as much as $\frac{1}{10}$. Tune in to your intuitive response and let a figure come to mind.

You sow the seed by donating it to a cause or venture with which you place value. Rather like sowing a seed in earth, you do not 'worry at it' by examining how it is being utilized, but rather let it go and forget about it.

Every day afterwards, take some time to gather your creative energy by taking four deep breaths and offering your seed picture as a gift to the most creative resources within you . . . .

Then after this offering each day, recall the 'seed' picture of your desire and offer it again . . . to the same higher consciousness within yourself . . .

This practice will strengthen the picture and make it clearer as it nears the stage where it will take form . . . .

> *Until your seed bears its fruit . . . hold it close to you as a secret . . . any mention of its contents to another will spill its power to reach fruition . . .*
>
> *Wash out all your doubts . . . they can so discourage the subconscious that the daily rite will be interrupted and your fruit will 'wither on the vine' . . . Doubts are like weeds that take valuable nutrients from the earth and destroy the success of the harvest . . .*
>
> *As before, now allow your intuition to guide you towards your desired outcome . . . Be prepared for the unusual to take place . . . Do not refuse any route because it seems too unlikely . . . it may lead you, indirectly, to just where you need to go.*

Sowing a seed has to do with learning to trust in the process of timing, knowing when it is time to take further action and when it is time to wait. A mood of enjoyment and laughter contributes towards preparing an open, receptive and fertile or nurturing ground for those seeds.

For the most part, we rightly equate action with results. If we want something, we need to take action to get it. However, we may mistakenly give up our dreams through a sense of frustration if the results we want do not happen exactly when we want them. The journey to our goals may be a process with stages we could not initially anticipate. This process takes the time it needs to be fulfilled and completed.

How many of the following observations concerning time have you found to be true?

1. When you are absorbed in some activity, the time 'flies'.
2. As we get older, the passage of time 'accelerates'.
3. When you were confined to a classroom and lacked interest in the content of the class, you watched the clock for the finishing time.
4. In an office environment, you have experienced conflicting pressures on 'your' time.
5. Having a deadline for completing a project compels you to be more 'productive' within the time available.

6. Leaving things until the last minute presents you with a challenge and excitement (like occasionally allowing *just enough* time to catch a train, boat or plane).
7. Using time 'non-productively' can produce feelings of guilt if you are driven to achieve results.
8. Conversely, if you are an under-achiever, or sabotage your potential for fulfilment, you may 'abuse' your time, such as by taking on too many (and conflicting) commitments, or by being consistently late for appointments.
9. You may use your time based upon examples set by people close to you in your early life, such as timing for meals. This may be very satisfactory, unless this pattern conflicts with your personal preferences as an adult.

It may be that up until now, your perception of managing time has been primarily a linear, rational one. A certain set of tasks take a specific length of time to complete and so you can make a clear, logical plan of progression for a project or a defined outcome. However, if you are embarking on something, new and so far unknown to you, there will be unknown factors. In this case, it will assist you to combine your linear time planning with your intuitive inner knowing. Is the next action you have in your plan really the most effective and productive one to take now?

Your intuition may serve, if you are in any doubt, to clarify whether at any moment, you are in fact making the best use of 'your time'. We can become so wrapped up in a line of activity that we lose sight of our overall mission or purpose in life. Given the full picture, is our current pursuit the most productive use of our time? Your personal resource of wisdom, through your intuition, may give you some valuable insights.

Making the Best Use of Your Time

As before, this exercise is one in which you brainstorm with questions on a sheet of paper. Allow whatever questions come to mind and write them down as they surface. Do not attempt to answer the questions, just let them keep coming until there are no more. Then, put them to one side to incubate.

Be aware over the next few days of the answers that come to you in the course of your everyday life. Make any improvements if you wish. You may even find that the adjustments start gradually integrating into and improving the quality of your life, without you having to make any conscious effort. The example illustrates the kinds of question you might ask of yourself.

- How can I make the best use of my time?
- Am I already making the best use of my time?
- What improvements can I make?
- What really are my priorities?
- Am I giving my best time to my priorities?
- Is there anything stopping me from making changes to my routine?
- How would I be spending my time on an ideal day?
- How could I spend my time to gain the greatest fulfilment?
- How could I use my time to achieve the greatest happiness in my close relationships?
- How can I achieve more and better results in less time?
- What is the most rewarding use of my time? How can I do that more?
- How can I eliminate the habits that make poor use of my time?
- What other questions do I need to ask?
- Who can assist me in the most rewarding use of my time?
- How can I be gentle with myself in adjusting the limiting habits I have had for a long time?
- How can I make time my friend?
- How can I make time for more fun?

With skilled personal management, you may organize your life so that while you are busy achieving in one area, another is ticking over on a 'back burner', or incubating, as described in *Clear Away Blocks*. Alternatively, you may be a person who never seems to stop, never takes a breather from a steady stream of activity.

Either way, you will benefit from having to hand knowledge of those pursuits that would come under the theme of pure pleasure, your personal inventory of Treats and Rewards. If up to now you have been mainly success-driven in the worldly sense, you may have lost touch with all that you do for pleasure alone.

If one stage of a project is incubating, and you have the time, how would you choose to enjoy yourself? How might you reward yourself on completion of that stage? How could you encourage and treat yourself when life's challenges seem to be coming thick and fast?

Your Personal Inventory of Treats and Rewards

Your inventory can be very broad and include items that take from a little to a lot of time; that cost from nothing to perhaps whatever you can reasonably, or sometimes even unreasonably, afford; that you would do alone, or with others; indoors, or outdoors; that would involve travel to a different location; with your family and/or friends.

A main factor about Treats and Rewards is that they take you out of the normal run of your life, that they are special for you and different. Treats and Rewards are a way you can celebrate your life.

Below are just a few possibilities. To bring to mind more for yourself, reflect back over some of your most enjoyable memorable moments. Recall who you were with, where you were and those instants that were special.

In a notebook, make a list of 20 Treats and Rewards that could act as a frequent reminder to you. The fact is, whether life is going apparently well, or otherwise, for you, you are always worth being given a Treat or Reward. That perception of, or attitude towards, yourself will contribute to your experience of successful living.

- A trip to the circus, theatre, zoo, theme park, concert
- Going bowling, skating, hang-gliding
- Reading a good novel, watching a favourite video
- Soaking in a warm bath, having a long massage
- Drawing a flower, gazing at a sunset/sunrise
- Going out to dinner, a discotheque, a party
- Taking a long holiday
- Drinking champagne
- A weekend in Paris, Hawaii, Venice
- Going shopping for luxuries
- Writing yourself a poem

Imagine for a while a world in which we were at one, at peace, with ourselves and all those around us. The emotional issues that might at one time have concerned us were now the subject of jokes and laughter. We could view the world through a child's eyes, moving from point to point, one event flowing into the next, each so new and interesting that the past was forgotten and there was no time or space to contemplate any future. The loving of close family and friends so filled us that we knew all our needs were being more than provided.

Could this be a formula for successful living? If we could create such conditions in our lives that we were free simply to have fun, would that be an aim worth having? Is it even possible?

You might even argue that such an approach is 'self-indulgent', or in some way inappropriate, given that so many are suffering in the world. Does personal freedom to enjoy life indicate a lack of caring?

Part of suffering is sometimes equated with deprivation, lack of resources, particularly money. However, some of the most effective fundraising has come about when large numbers of us are simply having fun. Millions of dollars and pounds have been raised with imagination and enthusiasm, through sponsored runs, television appeals, rock concerts. Perhaps it is true to say that:

There is no shortage of supply
There is only a shortage of demand

If we are at one with the world around us, we might be sensitive both to the difficulties being encountered by our fellow human beings, and, even miraculously, in touch with a tremendous force field of positive resources. Within each of us, there may be a profound loving intention to fulfil ourselves to the best of our ability, to communicate our loving concern to others. How we express that loving intention may be unclear. Our communications may not accurately reflect a loving intention, may not be perceived as such. We may also fail to appreciate the loving intentions of those close to us, when their behaviour fails to meet our expectations.

Living successfully demands a clear, loving intention towards your life as a whole and that begins with a compassionate and forgiving attitude towards yourself. The loving compassion you extend towards yourself will expand beyond yourself towards others. The child like nature of your inner world, when treated with loving care, will co-operate with you in fulfilling your adult aims. As you develop and learn the skills of inner co-operation, you will discover the world around you 'co-operating' with your inner intent.

The next exercise is a game to play in co-operation with your inner child and your loving intention.

The Yes/No Game –
Asking For What You Want

The first part of this exercise involves going within yourself and appreciating the loving intention within you and all those with whom you will interact.

Relax your physical body and take a few deep breaths . . . Breathe out any physical, mental or emotional distractions . . . Close your eyes . . . Remove yourself from the activity of your day and bring a smile to your face . . . Imagine the sun shining inside you and warmth radiating through every part of your body . . .

Allow that warmth and light to radiate beyond the boundaries of your body . . . and out into the air around you . . .

Bring someone into that warmth . . . it could be a family member . . . a friend . . . or a stranger . . . As they relax in the presence of your warmth . . . notice how they reflect it back to you . . . It may be in something they say . . . or do..

Above all, notice in the radiant quality of the warmth you share, your appreciation of who they are . . . Observe their loving intention . . . and how it communicates itself to you..

Practise this process of observation with one or two more people . . . family . . . friend . . . stranger..

As you perceive the world of fellow humans as being warm and friendly towards you, any 'fear of rejection' dissolves. In that world, you can be free to risk asking for what you most want. Any response, yes or no, is free from offence, is always for you.

The response no might be seen as an invitation to find someone else more appropriate to participate with you. There may be a better time, or any other reason that you may not be aware of.

The next part of this game is to play at asking for what you want. You might choose to ask those people with whom you *interact most closely and risk asking for something you have not previously dared before. You might experiment asking for something that you want, but could not imagine anyone granting. You might ask for something tangible, a rose, an air ticket, a photograph; or affection, such as a hug, a back massage or time to go for a walk.*

Give the child within you permission to ask for what he/she most wants. The game is one of asking and receiving. Do not stop to be concerned about any refusals. Just move to the next request.

You might like to play this game for a day, even a weekend. Be aware that others may catch on to the spirit of the game. Be ready to give, if you want, when asked yourself.

You may discover in playing this game that giving and receiving, whether you are giver or receiver, is a source of great fulfilment for you. The absence of emotional demands and expectations releases a lightness in the quality of your exchange.

You might be considering the area of serving others in some capacity as a primary objective. Service is perhaps not inflicting our 'goodness' on others in need, but our being willing to offer ourselves as required, or requested. The act of giving and receiving cannot be separated and needs no reward. As we give freely and openly, we instantly receive our reward. In our willingness to receive what another has to give, we allow them the fulfilment of their giving.

As adults living in a complex world, we can improve the quality of our lives by learning to love, appreciate and include the child within us that knows how simply to have fun. Learning to give and receive from the child within us may lead us to a better understanding and appreciation of the child within others. This can become an upward spiral of fulfilment.

You may view the raising of your children as a 20-year, or even longer, journey. Loving the child within you is a lifelong process. In amongst all your aims and objectives, you may benefit from the discipline of that loving. Discipline will produce freedom, and with that freedom, more joy.

Simply Have Fun – Creative Visualization

Find the place where you will be most comfortable and undisturbed . . . Sit or lie down in such a way that your body is well supported, your muscles are perfectly relaxed and you can breathe deeply. Take in a few deep easy breaths . . . breathing in relaxation and peacefulness, breathing out any tensions, irritations or disturbances . . . Notice and simply observe any tight places in your body . . . any worries or concerns . . . let them go as you breathe out . . .

Take yourself to an ideal day in your childhood, or in the childhood you would have most liked to have had . . . Imagine the perfect sunny weather . . . blue sky . . . friendly fresh breeze blowing through your hair . . . the sounds of birds and laughter . . . the excitement inside you of having the freedom to come and go and do exactly whatever you please . . . This day is for you . . .and for you alone . . . Whatever you wish for . . . it is there for you . . . A new teddy? . . . It is yours . . . What colour is it? . . . How large? . . . How does it feel when you cuddle it? . . . A set of drums? . . . You can make as much noise as you like . . . Play them – isn't that fun? . . . Want to go fishing with a friend? . . . To a river or a beach or a lake? . . . What fishing tackle are you using . . . what bait? . . . Who is with you? . . . Do you talk together . . . or are you quiet?

Have you ever wanted to fly . . . like a plane, a space shuttle or a butterfly? You can do this too. Just take a deep breath . . . and take off into the skies . . . How does that feel? . . . Exciting . . . a little scary? . . . How does the world look beneath you? . . . What is it like to be so high up . . . away from the houses and roads . . . rivers and fields . . . oceans and mountains?

. . . Can you hear the air rushing past you? . . . Look below . . . and notice a magic island that is sparkling green and gold . . .in the middle of crystal clear seas . . . Take care . . . and land yourself gently on to this island . . . Notice how special you feel as you touch the ground . . . it is so soft to your feet . . . The air is a perfect temperature . . . you smell its delicate sweetness as you breathe in . . . and bathe in the bliss of being where you consider to be at peace, at home . . .

With greater feelings than ever before of freedom and enthusiasm . . . you begin to explore . . . This is the island where all your dreams come true . . . With a click of a finger . . . Or the blink of an eye . . . Right in front of you the car . . . or the house . . . or the wife/husband of your dreams . . . Your enthusiasm and joy know no bounds . . . Be now vividly with the person or object you have created . . . What do you see? . . . What can you hear? . . . How does this feel for you? . . . Are there any special scents . . . or tastes associated with what you now have? . . . It may be that what you experience now is greater confidence . . . in passing a test . . . in winning an award . . . coming first in a track event . . . Notice your satisfaction and fulfilment . . . and thank yourself for your patience and endurance in achieving your aim . . .

What other dreams do you receive vividly now? . . . Notice the details . . . and enjoy to the full having that experience . . . knowing your ability to create all that you want . . .

Breathe in very deeply . . . expand those good feelings . . . and breathe out with a sigh . . . Once again . . . breathe in deeply . . . expand those feelings some more . . . and gently let that breath go . . .

Very gently . . . and in your own timing . . . open your eyes and become once again aware of being in your room . . . very relaxed . . . and with those good feelings still alive inside of you . . .

While you are still relaxed and in touch with your visions, make any notes about those experiences while they are still fresh in your mind.

The adult 'you' always has conscious control, the last say, over what you choose to do and how you choose to do it. Appreciating and co-operating with the inner child does not mean subsiding into childish moods and behaviours. However, if those imbalances occur, the chances are that the inner child is needing some loving attention and clear direction once again.

Nadine Stair, quoted at the beginning of the chapter, concludes her poem:

> I've been one of those persons
> who never goes anywhere without a thermometer,
> a hot water bottle, a raincoat, and a parachute.
> If I had to do it again,
> I would travel lighter than I have.

> If I had my life to live over,
> I would start barefoot earlier in the spring
> and stay that way later in the fall.
> I would go to more dances.
> I would ride more merry-go-rounds.

> I would pick more daisies.

Chapter 7
Start Now!

You may have observed in your life so far that there has often been a gap between a good intention and an outcome successfully accomplished.

Right now you may be caught in the Procrastination-Frustration Dilemma (see Figure 7). You may be able to see and know what you want but you do not have it yet (Frustration). And you may know clearly some of the things you need to do, but are putting off doing them (Procrastination). One emotion seems to be pulling you forward, while the other is holding you in the past.

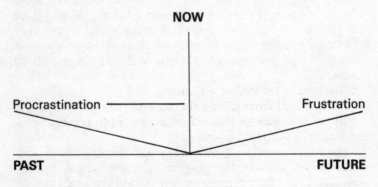

Figure 7: The Procrastination-Frustration Dilemma

As these emotions pull on you, even unconsciously, you are not free to enjoy what is immediately to hand. Unless you start directing your energy, taking action now, either to clear up matters from the past, or to take constructive steps towards the future vision you hold for yourself, you may find that the energies you have for accomplishment turn in on you and weigh you down.

One of the best ways to address this dilemma is to find and act on the initial steps that will either release the past or take you towards your vision.

In this chapter, you will have the opportunity to experiment with simple actions that may take no more than 10 minutes. In this way, you will gain the experiences of sampling different methods of producing a more successful lifestyle for yourself. Whatever reason or excuse you may come up with not to progress towards your dreams and visions, there will be probably at least one action you can take to overcome such an obstacle, before you finish reading this chapter.

The way it will work is this. As you have read through the book so far, you have probably had many thoughts and ideas about what you might do. The exercises in this chapter will be like mini Action/Productivity Cycles (from *Clear Away Blocks*). You will be able to translate your thought or idea into an action which you can do and finish in the next 10 minutes or so. The final stage of the cycle is to complete the action, and release more of your energy for the next step. Completion may take the form of acknowledging yourself in some way, or possibly evaluating the benefits you received from taking the action. This could be a statement that you record in a journal or notebook:

How I felt after taking action:

What I learnt from taking the action:

Any other comment that would be useful to remember in the future about taking action:

Given our unique combination of skills, talents and qualities, we all have the potential for adopting a creative approach to our lives. Creativity may start in our inner worlds of thinking and imagination. However, we are only truly 'creative' when we translate our thinking into tangible results or products through our physical activity.

Successful living then might be the healthy relationship between our inner world of experience, and our outer world of action and results.

Each chapter so far has addressed, in different ways, the question of clarifying what you want for yourself. Until you know what you want, it may be hard to get going. When you are clear, and enthusiastic, about what you want and are willing to do what it takes to get it, you may find yourself demonstrating capacities you had never imagined you possessed before.

In the review of the chapters that follows, have fun as you taste some of the sample actions on offer. Rather like tasting wine, it is not until you have had the experience that will you know the pleasure and satisfaction available to you.

Set Personal Objectives

The process of finding a vision and making it real

As a start, you might care to recall and reflect on some of your dreams and visions for the future. Considering a successful lifestyle, in your ideal world, what would you be experiencing and what would be happening for you and around you?

In *Set Personal Objectives*, we explored what motivates you from within and began the process of touching in to your innermost aspirations. You may have caught even a glimpse of a heartfelt desire, and temporarily pushed it to one side. We often do that. However, it is hard on ourselves to deny what in our heart of hearts we most deeply want because our innate life force is connected to those kinds of dreams. The choice can sometimes become either to enjoy the rewards of fulfilling the dream, or to suffer the pain of rejecting it.

A Step Nearer Your Dream

If you have an insight into what you want, you may well be experiencing a mixture of fear and excitement, doubt and awe. In other words, you may have a rush of energy and a blank mind as to what to do with it.

Glance through the following questions concerning your dream and choose one action that you will take now that will initiate your progress towards the dream.

What is your dream?

Is anyone else involved with you?

What skills will you use in achieving it?

What qualities will make you successful?

Who do you know that can assist you?

What inner resources will you need, or need to develop?

What outer resources will you require?

How will you have fun on the way?

What is your first simple, easy step, that you can take now, that will take less than 10 minutes?

For example:

- Make a phone call for information.
- Find the address of a person you need to write to and plan the letter.
- Write an affirmation for the main qualities you will need to fulfil your dream.
- Make an appointment to discuss your idea with the person who can best assist you with the initial stages.
- Research your sources of supply in Yellow Pages, list phone calls to make.

When you have taken your action, remember to evaluate how that was for you. You may even see clearly your next action.

You may be someone who is a good starter of projects, but a less good completer. Some of us are very good at having lots of ideas, but fall by the wayside when it comes to executing successfully any one of them. Your Personal Mission Statement may prove very valuable to you in sustaining your commitment until your safe arrival at your stated objectives. It may act as a guiding light that will tell you when you are out of alignment with your values and purpose in life.

Although your Personal Mission Statement may be written much like an Affirmation, it will be less those qualities which you now wish to strengthen and enhance, and more a reflection of who you are, the person you have always been. There is a continuity about your Mission or Life Purpose, although it may be expressed in different forms throughout the course of your life.

Acknowledge Your Mission

Remember that your Personal Mission Statement is best kept confidentially to yourself. Even disclosing it to a best friend or family member may lessen the value it could have for you. It may be that if you were 'accidentally' to let it slip, that Statement may not be the one for you.

In the next 10 minutes, take some action to enhance the inner experience of your Personal Mission Statement.

For example:

- Write it out in capital letters where you will see it often, such as in a diary.
- Close your eyes, and repeat it inwardly a few times, envisioning yourself living that Statement.
- Take a pad of paper and write it out, as many times as you can in 10 minutes.
- Write it out on an index or record card and put it where you can read it either first thing in the morning, or last thing at night.

● Complete the following statement in as many ways as you can in the next 10 minutes:

When I am fulfilling my purpose in life, I . . .

Complete the exercise with a positive evaluation and acknowledgement.

You may now be determining some specific goals for yourself. Before you finally commit your energy, effort and enterprise to any undertaking, consider the Triangle Of Fulfilment.

Working Your Triangle of Fulfilment

This is a simple formula for fulfilment where the three sides of a triangle represent:

● thought
● feeling
● action

as shown in Figure 8.

Figure 8: The Triangle of Fulfilment

For every thought you have, and feeling that matches it, you *take action* to bring about the result. Many of us have an inspired thought, with all the emotional impact of enthusiasm for it, but fail to follow through with the discipline of action which is required to make it happen.

Alternatively, we may have a good idea and attempt to put it into motion, but find we lack the emotive energy of enthusiasm to complete it. Or, we may have a lot of enthusiasm and launch ourselves into an activity without having properly thought it through.

In any venture or goal you are contemplating, make sure that you have the clear thought, with a strong positive feeling, and finally are willing to take the action required to produce fulfilment for yourself.

Look through any goals that you are considering. If any of them do not come into alignment for you, mentally, emotionally or in terms of the action you will need to take to complete them, decide now that they are already 'complete' for you.

In the next 10 minutes, do whatever you need to do to 'cross it off your list'. You may throw out a file with notes relating to that goal; tell yourself that you are no longer pursuing it; make a phone call and cancel an appointment you now no longer need.

You might like to complete this action by writing a statement, beginning:

I learnt . . ..

The result of this exercise will be that either you have cleared a space for a more fulfilling course of action, or you will have increased your commitment to fulfil the goal.

For example:

You may feel a rush of excitement and enthusiasm to write a novel; to see your words in print, your name on the book cover and receiving a small fortune in royalties. However, you have not thought through the work required to produce a book and the element of chance involved in having a first novel sell well.

'I learnt that although I would love to be a writer, when I thought about it more, I don't want to do all the work that is involved.'

Alternatively, you might be able to see very clearly how to establish a successful small business, know the steps involved and be able to make a very well-thought-through plan of action. However, you lack the passion and fundamental enthusiasm to sustain you in translating the good idea into a working reality.

'I learnt that although I really know how to make a business work successfully, I don't want to do that any more.'

Most of us do not plan to fail; we simply fail to plan.

If you are hesitant about embarking on your goals, you may not yet have defined clearly enough for yourself the specific series of steps, the actions required to achieve your result. Your head may be swimming with ideas and a feeling of pressure to get going but confusion about what needs to be done. At this point, an overview of what you are proposing to do will assist you to see the full picture, and you will be in a better position to plan all the details that will need your attention.

You may be a person who finds list-making a good way to plan a course of action. Our minds however 'think' by association rather than in a linear form of listed points.

When you are looking at a project, for example, moving house, establishing a voluntary activity in your community, changing your eating habits, writing a biography, passing an exam or going on a trekking holiday in the Himalayas, you will find it helpful to draw yourself a Mind Map. This will enable you to discover both what you already know, and the gaps in your current knowledge for which you will need to undertake some research.

Thorough research at the outset of a potential project may ultimately save you considerable time and energy.

Mind Map – A Step Towards Clarity

Take a blank sheet of paper and write your objective in the centre of the paper, with a circle around it. Bring to mind, in the form of headings, the areas associated with your objective that you will need to address in order to progress it. Draw a line out from the circle, with a heading on it.

There may be other thoughts you have associated with that heading, so draw lines from that original with the connected thoughts written on them, one thought per line. Carry on around your circle, with all the headings and the thoughts associated with them.

What you will have is a picture of what you already know. This could include some questions, or gaps, that you need to research or for which you need some assistance or guidance.

One of your first steps could be to fill in the gaps, to get the information or support you need. Knowing the questions you need to ask in any creative, or problem-solving situation, is a major contributing factor in achieving your results. The answers are always available to us, but we must know which questions to ask.

Alternatively, you may see very clearly where your priorities are and which area needs addressing first of all. Figure 9 illustrates how a Mind Map may look.

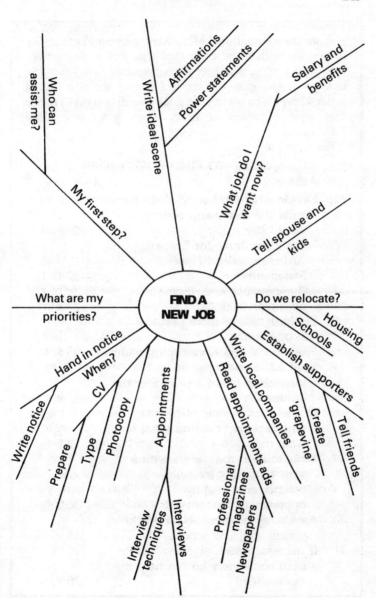

From the associational Mind Map, a linear Plan may be drawn up with some estimated Due Dates. Remember that your timing is at best a good guess. Any timetable is a set of guidelines to remind you of the best logical order of events to get to your goal. You may wish to revise this after a period of time, when you have more information.

For example:

GOAL: TO FIND A NEW JOB

	Actions	Due dates
1.	Decide what job I want to do now	15.8
2.	Decide the salary and benefits I would like	20.8
3.	Write Programme for Success, Affirmations and Power Statements	27.8
4.	Tell my spouse and discuss relocation options	22.8
5.	Establish one or more personal supporters	
6.	Prepare CV and have copies made	25.8
7.	Read ads in newspapers and magazines to get a picture of the job market	15.9
8.	Create a 'grapevine' of friends who can help me find what I want	22.9
9.	Write to local companies with a view to getting interview practice and creating opportunities for myself	30.9
10.	Assess my progress so far and re-valuate my next actions	15.10
11.	If necessary, seek objective advice from someone who can help me move ahead	20.10

Actions	Due dates
12. Take next actions	Not yet known
13. Repeat steps 10 to 12 until . . .	
14. Receive and accept job offer	30.11 ideally
15. Hand in notice to present job	1.12
16. Thank people who have assisted me	6.12
17. Celebrate with a bottle of champagne	10.12

This exercise has probably taken you rather more than 10 minutes. However, now that you have some specific steps outlined, why not choose one to do now to get you moving? It could be a first phone call, outline for your CV or a proposed job description for yourself.

If you have done all parts of this exercise, you might like to complete it for yourself with an acknowledgment, or a small reward of some kind.

Preparation and planning will assist you in minimizing mistakes. Perhaps one of the greatest benefits of clear planning and logical evaluation is that of keeping your mind open and receptive to your intuitive leads and guidance. Both the practical, logical side of your nature, and the more imaginative, can work hand in hand.

Unlock Your Attitude

The power of positive focusing.
If you were driving a car, you would focus on the road ahead of you, not on the rear-view mirror. As you focus your attention ahead of you on your visions, objectives and goals, you will find your future is determining your present experience. We explored in *Unlock Your Attitude* how, no matter

what hardships or difficulties have beset you in the past, they no longer need inhibit you in the present.

As you embark on a new direction in your life, it is likely that you may encounter some obstacles before you achieve your aims. However, the main obstacles to your progress are within you, and within your power to overcome.

It is within the inner worlds of our attitudes and beliefs that we have the greatest influence. As we open the doors to an improved quality of lifestyle and new avenues for expression, we can, in each moment, choose to expand into the new direction, or contract towards a more limiting experience. Your power to choose the most positive, uplifting perspective in any circumstance will contribute towards both the success of your journey and the successful arrival of your objectives.

One of the surest signs that you have lost a greater perspective of life, or your objectivity, is when you have lost your sense of humour.

Do not take life too seriously; you will never get out of it alive.

Why not take a laughter break from time to time? Recall a funny incident that still makes you laugh, or read some jokes, even corny ones can make you smile. Our limiting beliefs may cause us to doubt ourselves on some level. What if, however, we could see the funny side of some of our negative attitudes? This might release us from them and put them in their place.

Entertaining Your Limiting Belief

Our limiting beliefs or attitudes are really thin and fragile in relation to the inner strengths that sustain us. In this brief exercise, explore the lighter side of a belief that may stand more than anything else in the way of achieving a more successful lifestyle.

First of all, bring an important objective, dream or vision to mind.

Now think of the attitude or belief you hold that would *most* get in the way of your achieving it.

In your imagination, expand the limitation until it has become absurd, ridiculous and unbelievably funny.

Draw a diagram or cartoon to illustrate the attitude or limiting belief at its most bizarre.

Complete the exercise with a statement in a journal or notebook about any new perspective you gained towards any limitations you may have held.

The example below illustrates this exercise:

The limiting belief is that if I say what it is I really want, people will laugh at me and I will look incredibly foolish. And that scares me a lot.

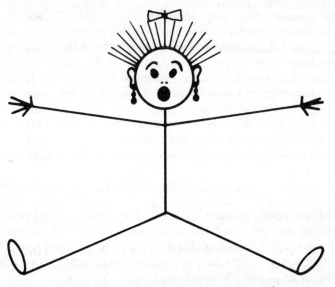

The cartoon is me looking really foolish with my hair standing on end and having a terrified expression. The terror is grossly out of proportion with my asking for the pay rise which has already been mentioned.

One of the most effective methods of turning a mood of restriction into fresh inspiration is to experience and communicate to another person your sense of appreciation.

Gratitude – Being Thank-Full

Without moving from where you are now, cast your mind over your life so far. Who is the person who has contributed the most to you, up to now? There may be more than one that you can think of. However, for the purpose of this exercise, pick one and bring to life the feeling of gratitude you have for the gifts this person has given you.

Choose one way in which you would like to communicate your appreciation to this person. If you can speak to them directly, do that; or you could phone; write a brief letter or card, and send it. If the person is no longer alive, you can still write the letter.

However you would like to do it, take a few minutes now to do this exercise.

Complete the exercise by evaluating any results you experienced, inwardly, or outwardly.

A final brief exercise for gaining a fresh perspective is one that involves physical movement. Our bodies are designed for perhaps much greater mobility than we typically utilize. Fatigue and weariness may be brought on more by lack of physical action than excess of it. Have you ever found that after a strenuous bout of exercise, you have become more energized and seem to need less sleep?

It is possible that some of the limitations we hold against ourselves get reflected in areas of the physical body as various forms of tension, or even 'dis-ease'. Even a 10-minute exercise break may give you the fresh perspective you need on some issue or concern.

Move – And Gain A New View

Take the next 10 minutes to do any kind of physical exercise. You might go for a brisk walk, do jumping jacks, dance to some music, find a rope and skip with it, run on the spot.

Complete this exercise by noting any observations you made in a journal or notebook.

Clear Away Blocks

Transforming obstacles into resources

To gain clarity, power and purpose you can take action in many ways to transform that which seemingly stands in your path. The greatest apparent block may turn into your greatest resource, including information and understanding that was previously concealed from you.

Broadly speaking, blocks fall into two areas:

1. Deadwood – outstanding, unresolved matters from the past which hold you back there.
2. Resistance – as you anticipate improvements, you mentally and emotionally resist changing habitual behaviours, routines and beliefs (Comfort Zones and Self-Image).

Whatever you have been doing in your life so far has been giving you the results you are getting. If you want to produce a different experience, you need to *do* something different.

Transforming your lifestyle may well require that you undergo significant personal transformation. Confronting the inner resistance to change can be made easier by taking it in small, manageable chunks. It is best not to fight the resistance but to make passing through the Comfort Zones as effortless as possible.

Clearing Deadwood is perhaps the most tangible and rewarding activity for gaining energy and inspiration. In the next exercise, see what you can accomplish, in terms of your well-being, taking 10 minutes or less to deal with an outstanding issue. Think for a moment about splinters of wood. Even though they are small, they inflict pain when they catch in our skin.

Clearing Out The Splinters

A splinter is a piece of deadwood that will take no longer than 10 minutes to clear, probably less. Look around you and notice something you have been meaning to do for a long time and which has now become a source of dread, frustration or irritation. By-pass any reluctance you may have and handle it now.

Below are some examples of splinters:

- write your letter of resignation
- clear out a file/drawer/shelf
- make a dental appointment
- invite mother-in-law for dinner
- open the letter from the bank manager

Put this book down. Take the action. Complete it by observing how you felt and record the benefits you gained from doing it.

Handling one splinter like this may well encourage you to do another. If so, why not do it now, before reading on?

For many of us, money is at some time a major issue that seems to hold us back and usually, but not always, the shortage of it rather than an excess. However, is the apparent security of a monthly salary and job benefits standing in the way of your pursuing personal fulfilment?

Your Money – Asset or Liability?

In order to begin addressing the issue of money, it will help to be as relaxed, open and receptive as possible. If the subject makes you feel nervous, take a few deep breaths and tell yourself to relax. No one is looking over your shoulder as you explore the following questions.

Are you tied to a job or some other circumstance in your life in which the main rewards are material, rather than personally fulfilling?

Is the financial payoff worth the sacrifice in terms of your vitality and enjoyment of life?

Are there any debts that you need to pay off to move ahead clearly in your life?

Do you need to make a plan and communicate to your creditors what you intend to do?

Is there anyone who can assist you to do this?

Have you taken stock of **all** your material assets?

Are there any 'nest eggs' you may have forgotten about?

What are your financial needs?

Would it assist you to consult with someone who can make sure you include all items, in a budget if necessary?

What else do you need to know and do now to clarify any apparent financial restraints that are in the way of your achieving your Superlife?

Observe any answers to the above questions as they occur to you.

If your financial block concerns money you owe, take action now to make a necessary phone call, write a letter, pay an overdue account.

If you are attached to excessive financial security, at the expense of your personal fulfilment, find a worthwhile cause and write a cheque as a donation.

Complete the exercise by noting the benefits you experienced from doing the exercise.

Consider now any emotional blocks you may have towards changing a familiar routine, habitual pattern of behaviour or thinking that is now in conflict with your objectives for a successful lifestyle. You may need to sacrifice 30 minutes in bed in the morning in order to begin a daily meditation practice. Or, you may need to eat more salads, and less ice cream and chocolate, to gain a new bodyweight. To become a good manager, you may need to learn how to delegate and work with a team. To write a novel, you may need to develop self-discipline.

Whatever the block, consider it your friend. In this next exercise, open a dialogue with whatever you view as your greatest block and allow it to serve you.

Making Friends With Your Block

This may take you a little longer than 10 minutes but will prove well worth your investment of time. The aim of the dialogue between 'you' and 'the block' is to discover one small step that will lead you beyond it.

Identify your greatest block to progressing (e.g. fear, stubbornness, resentment, procrastination, boredom, fatigue).

Open the dialogue with the following two questions:
1. What are the qualities you see that I have and how do you see me withholding them?
2. What are the qualities you see that you have, and how are you withholding them?

And let the block (e.g. fear) respond:

Fear: I notice that you have a lot of enthusiasm for your

objectives, but you are using me as an excuse not to perform. The qualities I have for you are to make sure you don't rush into something without looking carefully where you are going. I don't withhold my qualities, but sometimes, I come on a bit strong.

Me: The thing I need to do next is tell my brother that I cannot stay in the business partnership with him. I can see how angry he will be with me and you are holding me back from making that move. Can you help me with this?

Fear: On the face of it, he might be angry. But you two have not been getting on. He could be relieved when you talk to him. Why not make some time to listen to his point of view, and explain to him what you are wanting to do now?

Me: That makes sense. I could now arrange a time for us to talk. Is there any other advice you can give me? . . . .

When your block delivers a solution that you can begin to effect now, act on it immediately.

Complete the action with a positive evaluation and acknowledge yourself in some way for having taken it.

Confronting obstacles and meeting the challenges presented by your new vision will be made much easier by having one or more others to stand by you and hold the picture of your success. In your moments of weakness, your team can throw you a lifebelt of encouragement and reassurance that will see you to the winning line.

Choosing Your Supporters

Reflect on your goals and objectives. What are some of the challenges you can anticipate now on the way to achieving them? Are there any particular gaps in your knowledge or experience to date which another person can fill in for you? Is there a specific area of expertise with which you would like to receive assistance?

Who are the people you know who can best act as your friends and allies? This could be close friends, or family members. It could also be a professional adviser in some capacity, someone for whose services you pay a fee.

Make a list of your potential supporters now. Select one person. Now, write to let him/her know what you are planning, and how he/she might be able to assist you, or phone and arrange a time when you can meet up to discuss your plans.

Complete the exercise by acknowledging any benefits you received from it.

If we want *more* in our lives, we may need to let go of that which is the *lesser*: for more wealth, release attitudes of poverty; for more loving, release anger and resentment; for more time, release time-wasting thinking, behaviours and activities. As you let go, allow yourself to celebrate the passing.

Create Inner Strength

Nurturing self-confidence and encouragement
You are your own best resource. The actions you take to nurture yourself will pay you great dividends.

It is likely that the more powerful and inspiring your vision, or objectives for yourself, the greater will be the demand on your personal resources. This is perhaps both the good news and the bad news.

The good news is that the more you draw on your deepest reserves, the greater will be your inner rewards. The bad news (which is not really so bad) is that it may not be easy for you. You will be stretched beyond, at times, what you think is possible.

Consider the example of the three-year-old toddler who successfully learnt to swim with the aid of air-filled arm bands. As her confidence grew, her aunt gradually let the air out of the arm bands so that finally she was swimming with empty arm bands. However, when the arm bands were removed and she was put back into the swimming pool, she sank. The empty arm bands were put on again, and she swam confidently once more.

Whenever we are in the process of learning new skills as we grow into a more successful lifestyle, we too may need the equivalent of air-filled arm bands as a temporary support. We do not need to cast aside our support systems in advance of our being ready to do so.

We cannot be too kind to ourselves. The kindness, tenderness and compassion that we can demonstrate towards ourselves gets extended out to others, and eventually returned to us in many unexpected forms. Your demonstration of a successful lifestyle can be the cornerstone for the next person's experience of success. To become a part of that upward spiral in your life may be the most thrilling adventure you could ever wish to undertake.

A new successful lifestyle begins with loving who you are now; valuing what you now have and have in front of you to do. Take a few minutes now to nurture your inner being.

Affirmation – Mirror Work

This is a powerful way of using affirmations to touch you most deeply. Our inner strength is perhaps most called upon in challenging personal relationships when we may possibly lead ourselves to doubt our innate goodness.

For this exercise, think of three areas in which you sabotage yourself with limiting attitudes in personal relationships. Then, write down what you would tell yourself to affirm a corresponding positive quality, like an Affirmation but written in the second person.

Now, look into a mirror and tell yourself, silently or aloud, the qualities that you truly are. Experiment with saying the words as if you fully mean them.

For example:

Your negative beliefs might be that you are unattractive, dull and fundamentally unlovable.

In this case, you might wish to affirm to yourself in front of a mirror something like the following:

- You are bright and attractive
- You are fun and lively
- You are a kind and loving person
- You are a great friend
- You are simply wonderful

Complete the exercise by noticing any subtle changes in how you feel, having done it.

One of the ways we can best strengthen our self-confidence is to fulfil the commitments we have made with ourselves. Often, as a result of the demands on our time and attention, we neglect or forget to honour the promises we have made to ourselves. You may recall having a conversation with your inner child. Return to your inner child now for the next exercise.

Relax – and Love Who You Are

Take a few deep breaths and imagine yourself surrounded by a peaceful, clear white light. In a brief dialogue with your inner child, find out if there are any areas you may have neglected, that you have promised yourself, but not yet carried out.

You may do this exercise mentally, or perhaps better, written out. For example:

Alice: The past few weeks, I have been very busy and have not taken the time to see how you are doing.

Little Alice: I had noticed that.

A You sound a little fed up.

LA Yes, I am. Seems like we've had no fun recently.

A Is there anything I have overlooked?

LA You did say we would go riding horses one afternoon and we haven't done that yet. Did you forget?

A No, but I will call the stables right now and arrange a time. How about that?

LA Great!

A Which horse would you like to ride? I will make sure that one is available . . .

When you have identified any omissions, if possible make a phone call immediately, or write a letter or make a note in your diary now to take the appropriate action.

Whatever you may agree to do in your dialogue, make sure you complete that action.

Developing your inner strength may take paying attention to some seemingly very small details. What may not rate as a priority, in terms of the goals and objectives you consider important in the outer world, may have great significance in your well-being and peace of mind. The number of 'small' details actively cared for may measurably increase the inner quality of your life.

Expect Success

Progressing to success with ease

Creating and affirming detailed images of success within you will make achievement happen more easily. Having placed the picture of fulfilment into your unconscious makeup, you then need to watch for the signs that show when you may be going off track, and those which confirm that you are heading in the right direction.

One of the best indicators that will catch your attention is the language you use, both in thinking and in speaking. This is because a negative thought will likely show up as some form of tension, or lack of ease, in your body.

How often have we resolved to change a pattern of behaviour, such as over-eating or smoking, and 'resolved' to start 'next Monday', or 'after Christmas'. Why not start your language diet right now?

Watch Your Words

Think about some of the expressions you use frequently which may have a negative, if subtle, tone to them. By using what are known as:

generalizations

distortions

deletions

we may unwittingly be deceiving ourselves, and others. Language deficits will weaken our resolve for accomplishing our dreams.

For example:

It's the last straw. (Is it?)

Bad things happen to good people. (Always?)

I'm never on time. (Not once?)

Today's not my day. (Whose day is it?)

I just can't . . . (Or don't really want to?)

The exercise to do now is to bring just one such phrase to mind which you have used against yourself in some way.

Write a Power Statement now that will create a new pattern of thought, and possibly behaviour. Write it out 10 times now, repeating the words aloud as you write them.

For example:
Challenges bring out my greatest resources.
Everything that comes to me is for me.
It's fun to be early for my appointments.
I make my days work for me.
I always can when I want to . . .

You may notice in days to come that you will know very clearly if and when you go off your diet. You will feel better, more energized, for sticking to it.

Complete the exercise with any observations you may have made in doing it.

Money

As long as we are using money as our medium of exchange for goods and services, it will doubtless play a part in the question of what living successfully means for us. How many of us are really in charge of our lives when it comes to money? Our emotions seem to get invested in it, one way or another, and thus it becomes a source of disturbance.

In an earlier exercise, we looked at how money might be holding you back. In this next exercise, we can sow the seeds of a much healthier relationship with money, in which it ceases to be a source of concern and becomes the utility it is.

Money In Your Superlife

Cast your mind forward to your new experience of a successful lifestyle. Within it, consider the part that money will be playing, and your relationship with your financial circumstances.

Allow yourself to come up with five Power Statements that describe positively the role that money plays in your Superlife.

For example:

- I always have enough for what I really want to do.
- I enjoy paying my bills easily each month.
- I am grateful for having peace of mind concerning money.
- I enjoy being able to give donations to charity.
- I experience great freedom in relation to money.

Now choose just one of those Power Statements and take some action that matches the Statement.

For example:

Send that donation to charity, it need not be huge.

Be clear about a small something you really want and, if you have the money at your disposal, write a cheque now to have it, or do it.

Leave some change in a telephone kiosk for the next person.

Send a gift of flowers anonymously.

Give your cab driver an extra large tip.

Leave money in a parking meter for the next car.

Complete this exercise by acknowledging your willingness to address what may have given you mixed feelings in the past.

There is no great mystery to achieving a successful lifestyle. Each experience of your life so far, positive or negative, will have provided you with information about the constituents of success. Remember that, as you expect success, you may now:

1. Do more of what works for you.
2. Do less of what does not work for you.
3. Experiment with new methods of producing an even greater experience of your successful lifestyle.

Simply Have Fun

Life is simple, life is fun – enjoy it!
You will find that having enjoyment and pleasure as you progress towards your objectives is just as valuable to you as the final arrival at your destination, possibly even more so. In those moments when we are relaxed and having fun we receive inner knowing 'out of the blue', moments of clarity when we feel at one with ourselves and the world.

Consider the qualities that you have, that you can enjoy more now. Consider the qualities that perhaps you like less, and see how at times, they are really funny. Some of the best humour comes out of our perceived tragedy or misfortune.

You have cause for celebration. Celebrate the life that is you, celebrate the many gifts with which you were born, but which perhaps you have yet to realize fully.

Celebrate Your Life – Celebrate You

Who you are is magnificent. The life force, the spirit that is the source of your vitality in each moment is so extraordinary and yet maybe you have only had glimpses of it up to now.

You could well have riches available to you, however accomplished you have been in your life to date, that are way beyond the present scope of even your wildest dreams. The riches you produce in the world are but a fraction of the riches of your inner spirit.

Choose this day for your celebration. You can make it like a birthday if you like. This birthday is one of awakening more fully to the magnificence of who you are. It can be celebrated annually, or more often if you like.

The first part of this exercise is an inner one, one in which you capture the magnificence of who you are. You will need to ask for the permission of your inner child to co-operate and play with you fully.

Breathe deeply and relax your body . . . Close your eyes and

tune inwardly to your heart centre, the centre of your chest . . .
Breathe in a white light through the centre of your forehead
. . . and breathe out a warm pink light from your heart centre
. . . As you breathe in and out . . . envisage yourself being
perfectly surrounded and protected by this pink loving energy
. . .

In your creative imagination . . . take yourself to the most
magnificent palace in the richest kingdom of all time and space
. . . Look at the beauty of its surroundings . . . the splendour
and detail of its structure . . . the colour and form of the front
door . . . as it opens out towards you to welcome you in . . .

Feel the excitement as you step forward and stand in awe of
the light and texture of the hallway . . . the feel of the ground
beneath your feet . . . the sounds of music in the air . . . As
you walk through the rooms . . . you feel a magic . . . a sense
of wonder at all you see around you . . . It is almost as though
your breath is taken away . . . For as you take in the fullness
of all that you perceive . . . there is also a great peace and
stillness inside you . . .

Breathe into the peace and stillness . . . Expand it now so
that every cell in your body is filled . . . filled with the
splendour of who you are . . .

Maintaining those good feelings . . . open your eyes once
again . . . and become aware of your body . . .

Now you can decide how you will celebrate your special day.
You might like to use a Mind Map as a step towards planning
the best day of your life so far . . .

What would you most like to do? Who would you like to
celebrate with? Would you like to announce your birthday in
some way? What gift(s) would you like to receive? Is there a
special place you would like to spend your day? Is there any
treat you would particularly like to have? Would you like a party
with friends, or dinner with a loved one?

Allow some time to plan whatever you would like. To
complete your planning, affirm to yourself, at least once, in a
mirror:

I love you.
This may be the most challenging task for you to contemplate.
Give yourself permission to do it, nevertheless, because you might find it very rewarding.
Now go out and actively make the Happy Birthday of your dreams come true.

Start Now

It's hard by the yard; it's a cinch by the inch . . . and even silly millimetres will do.

The place to start living successfully is within you. And that you can do now, and in each subsequent moment. Each choice made consciously in your favour will be reflected in some aspect of your life outwardly. Turn on the light to your life as a precious adventure.

Start Now – A Resolution

Superlife is a process of expansion, of growing into the fulfilment of your lifetime resources.

This exercise will illustrate to you what you can do, from moment to moment. You might like to keep it somewhere as a reference. The idea here is not that you blame yourself in any way if you slip from your best intentions. Simply return to your heart centre, pick one of the central themes of your resolution and act now on it in some way.

In the centre of a blank page, draw a heart. If you have not drawn many hearts, this comes with practice. The heart is a reminder to you of your source of inner strength, courage, inspiration and many other qualities that sustain you.

In the heart shape, write:
I will start now . . .
and around the heart, draw lines with what you will do to re-connect with your source of wisdom.
Example:

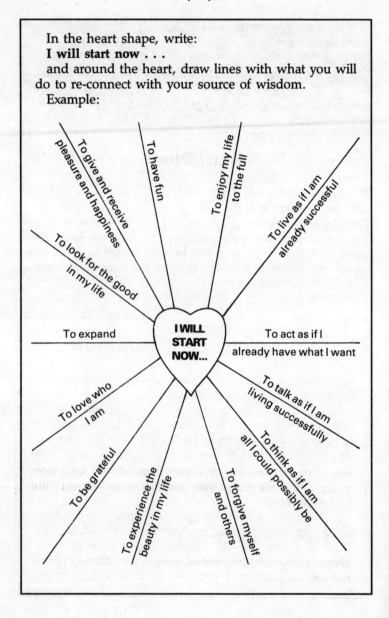

You might also care to have the following summary as a reminder to yourself.

Superlife – Approach With Care

1. Acceptance

Progressing into your Superlife may involve some ups and downs, physically, mentally and emotionally. These are a healthy part of transition.

2. Loving

Ask for the love, support and listening ear of family and friends. Be open to their points of view, but not necessarily advice, unless it is clear and objective, leaving you complete choice of further action.

3. Take Positive Action

- Nurture yourself on all levels
- Generate laughter, enjoyment and fun
- Express gratitude and appreciation to yourself
- Take regular physical exercise
- Discard personal effects of no further value

4. Vision Ahead

Keep your attention directed forward on long-term visions or objectives that inspire your interest and enthusiasm.

5. Plan for Pleasure

Create your own daily encouragement by having plenty to look forward to positively, such as special treats.

6. Be Patient and Relax

The process of achieving your Superlife may take time. Excessive pressure on, demands and expectations of yourself may be counterproductive and delay positive outcomes.

7. Above All . . .

. . . **be loving** to yourself. Be aware of the blessings which may be coming in temporary disguises.

We are each of us born with extraordinary gifts, talents and abilities, and yet how many of us live to realize fully all that we have available to us? Once you know, and play in tune, with who you are, worlds of delight will open up for you. However you choose to play, know that you can choose to experience a successful lifestyle. Life is for successful living.

Embrace your SUPERLIFE!

Of further interest . . .

THE TRUTH ABOUT SUCCESS AND MOTIVATION
DR BOB MONTGOMERY

If you want to be successful – at work, at play, in love or as a parent then this book is for you. Dr Bob Montgomery offers straightforward advice that will help you achieve a balanced lifestyle with success in every field.

Do you believe that success means beating others? If you do, Dr Montgomery shows you that you *must* fail. The mark of a successful person is someone who recognizes exactly what success is *for them*; someone who knows that they can succeed best through co-operation, not competition.

There is very little sense in being a success in one field if the rest of your life is a dismal failure; the basis of success is planning, and running, a balanced lifestyle. Dr Montgomery shows you how to set your own realistic goals. His tips for acquiring the skills needed to succeed include:
- How to motivate yourself and others
- How to communicate and negotiate
- How to resolve conflict and manage anger
- How to solve problems and assert yourself

Dr Bob Montgomery runs a consultancy for individuals and for business and industry based in Melbourne, Australia.

A WHACK ON THE SIDE OF THE HEAD
ROGER VON OECH

- Be foolish
- Break the rules
- Make mistakes
- Take risks
- Expect the unexpected
- Ask what if . . .?
- Follow your intuition
- See the big picture

The secret of being more creative is to be able to look at the world in a different way. This book, an international bestseller, will 'whack' you out of your traditional thought patterns and set your creative self free.

Fully illustrated, filled with provocative puzzles, anecdotes, exercises, cartoons, quotations, questions, stories and tips . . . you can learn how to refresh your outlook and start thinking in new, creative ways.

Roger von Oech runs a California-based consulting firm. He has conducted highly successful creativity seminars with companies such as American Express, Apple Computers, Coca-Cola, IBM and Procter & Gamble.

THE CALM TECHNIQUE
PAUL WILSON

Close your eyes and you will see clearly
Cease to listen and you will hear truth
TAOIST POEM

Of all the techniques to enhance health, happiness and harmony, meditation is one of the most effective and easy to learn. This practical introduction explains:

- The nature of meditation
- The nature of the stress problems meditation can solve
- A step-by-step guide to how to meditate

The author has also included a variety of exercises, and a question and answer section, as well as some tips on other lifestyle techniques to enhance the effectiveness of meditation. Simply by giving yourself 30 minutes a day, you will be able to ease stress, improve your sex-life, and generate self-confidence.

WHAT TO SAY WHEN YOU TALK TO YOUR SELF

SHAD HELMSTETTER

You don't have to be crazy to talk to yourself!

We all talk to ourselves all of the time, usually without realising it. And most of what we tell ourselves is negative, counterproductive and damaging . . . preventing us from enjoying a fulfilled and successful life.

Shad Helmstetter's simple but profound techniques, based on an understanding of the processes of the human brain, have enabled thousands of people to get back in control of their lives.

By learning how to talk to yourself in new ways, you will notice a dramatic improvement in all areas of your life. You will feel better and accomplish more. It will help you achieve more at work and at home, lose weight, overcome fears, stop smoking and become more confident. And it works.

Shad Helmstetter, Ph.D, is a bestselling author of many personal growth books, and the leading authority in the field of Self-Talk.

YOU CAN'T AFFORD THE LUXURY OF A NEGATIVE THOUGHT

PETER McWILLIAMS
and JOHN-ROGER

Negative thinking can damage your health!

It is one of the most serious diseases of our time, obstructing us from believing that we really *deserve* happiness: an attitude which affects us mentally, physically, and emotionally. Negative thinking can provide the right environment for illness to prosper. How important it is, then, for those with serious illnesses *not* to indulge in it.

The cure is simple. *Savour* the positive in your life; weed out the negative; *enjoy* each moment. The path is not easy but this best-selling book will infect you with its sense of fun and its gregarious wisdom. Packed with inspirational quotes it will unlock new possibilities in your life as well as being both compelling and uplifting reading. Accept *your* right to live life to the full!

MIND TRAPS
TOM RUSK and NATALIE RUSK

Mind Traps are those self-delusions which keep you locked into unsatisfactory habits, relationships and situations. But because you are your own worst enemy, you can't see where you're going wrong. In this book, Tom Rusk offers you a complete self-change programme which you tailor to your own needs. You will learn to look at yourself objectively and identify the particular traps which are holding you back. These might include:

- The Self Doubt Trap
- The Fear of Failure Trap
- The Conceit Trap
- The Shy and Lonely Trap
- The Jealousy Trap
- The Perfectionist Trap

Let this programme set you free from your mind traps, and free from yourself – it will help you to change your mind, and your life!